TREE-FRINGED FAUKE LAKE, NEAR ANCHORAGE

THE SHORE OF THE BEAUFORT SEA, PART OF THE ARCTIC OCEAN

ICEBERGS BEACHED AT WACHUSETT INLET IN GLACIER BAY

MOUNTAIN GOATS ON A COASTAL MOUNTAINSIDE

NORTH SLOPE TUNDRA BURNISHED WITH FALL COLORS

RUSSIAN JACK SPRINGS STEAMING IN SUB-ZERO COLD

Other Publications:

UNDERSTANDING COMPUTERS
THE ENCHANTED WORLD
YOUR HOME
THE KODAK LIBRARY OF CREATIVE PHOTOGRAPHY
GREAT MEALS IN MINUTES
THE CIVIL WAR
PLANET EARTH
COLLECTOR'S LIBRARY OF THE CIVIL WAR
THE EPIC OF FLIGHT
THE GOOD COOK
THE SEAFARERS
WORLD WAR II
HOME REPAIR AND IMPROVEMENT
THE OLD WEST

For information on and a full description of any
of the Time-Life Books series listed above,
please write:
Reader Information
Time-Life Books
541 North Fairbanks Court
Chicago, Illinois 60611

*This volume is one of a series that explores the
wild regions of the United States, the
Caribbean, Mexico and Central America.*

WILD ALASKA

THE AMERICAN WILDERNESS/TIME-LIFE BOOKS/ALEXANDRIA, VIRGINIA

BY DALE BROWN
AND THE EDITORS OF TIME-LIFE BOOKS

Time-Life Books Inc.
is a wholly owned subsidiary of
TIME INCORPORATED

FOUNDER: Henry R. Luce 1898-1967

Editor-in-Chief: Henry Anatole Grunwald
President: J. Richard Munro
Chairman of the Board: Ralph P. Davidson
Corporate Editor: Jason McManus
Group Vice President, Books: Reginald K. Brack Jr.
Vice President, Books: George Artandi

TIME-LIFE BOOKS INC.
EDITOR: George Constable
Executive Editor: George Daniels
Editorial General Manager: Neal Goff
Director of Design: Louis Klein
Editorial Board: Dale M. Brown, Roberta Conlan,
Ellen Phillips, Gerry Schremp, Donia Ann Steele,
Rosalind Stubenberg, Kit van Tulleken, Henry Woodhead
Director of Research: Phyllis K. Wise
Director of Photography: John Conrad Weiser

PRESIDENT: William J. Henry
Senior Vice President: Christopher T. Linen
Vice Presidents: Stephen L. Bair, Edward Brash, Robert A.
Ellis, John M. Fahey Jr., Juanita T. James, James L. Mercer,
Wilhelm R. Saake, Paul R. Stewart, Leopoldo Toralballa

THE AMERICAN WILDERNESS
EDITOR: Charles Osborne
Editorial Staff for Wild Alaska
Text Editor: David S. Thomson
Picture Editor: Susan Rayfield
Designer: Charles Mikolaycak
Staff Writer: Gerald Simons
Chief Researcher: Martha T. Goolrick
Researchers: Terry Drucker, Margo Dryden,
Villette Harris, Myra Mangan,
Susanna Seymour, Molly E. C. Webster
Design Assistant: Mervyn Clay
Copy Coordinator: Eleanore W. Karsten
Picture Coordinator: Joan Lynch

Revisions Staff
EDITOR: Rosalind Stubenberg
Text Editor: Lee Greene
Researchers: Kristin Baker, Reiko Uyeshima
Copy Coordinator: Cynthia Kleinfeld
Art Assistant: Jeanne Potter
Picture Coordinator: Jane A. Martin
Editorial Assistants: Mary Kosak, Linda Yates

Editorial Operations
Design: Ellen Robling (assistant director)
Copy Chief: Diane Ullius
Editorial Operations: Caroline A. Boubin (manager)
Production: Celia Beattie
Quality Control: James J. Cox (director)
Library: Louise D. Forstall

CORRESPONDENTS: Elisabeth Kraemer-Singh (Bonn); Margot
Hapgood, Dorothy Bacon (London); Miriam Hsia, Susan
Jonas, Lucy T. Voulgaris (New York); Maria Vincenza
Aloisi, Josephine du Brusle (Paris); Ann Natanson (Rome).
Valuable assistance was also provided by: Mollie Bowditch
(Anchorage); Jesse Birnbaum (San Francisco).

The Author: Dale Brown, an editor for TIME-LIFE BOOKS, gathered material for this volume on three trips to Alaska. He traveled thousands of miles, from the Alaskan Panhandle in the south to Barrow, the northernmost point of the state. With a guide, he explored the arctic wilderness north of the vast Brooks Range. He made his first Alaskan visit while writing American Cooking: The Northwest for TIME-LIFE BOOKS' Foods of the World. He is also the author of American Cooking, The Cooking of Scandinavia and, for the TIME-LIFE Library of Art, The World of Velázquez.

The Consultant: William O. Pruitt Jr. is professor of zoology at the University of Manitoba in Winnipeg and a long-time student of animal life in Alaska. A native of Virginia who discovered he is happiest when the temperature is 20° below zero, he is an expert on the ecology of snow. In addition to his many professional papers and magazine articles he is the author of Animals of the North, a classic work on the subject, and Boreal Ecology.

The Cover: In the Brooks Range in northern Alaska, the midnight sun gleams on an unnamed mountain and an ice-choked tundra stream.

Library of Congress Cataloguing in Publication Data
Brown, Dale.
  Wild Alaska, by Dale Brown and the editors of Time-Life
Books. New York, Time-Life Books [1972]
  184 p. illus. (part col.) 27 cm. (The American wilderness)
  Bibliography: p. 180.
  1. Natural history — Alaska.   I. Time-Life Books.   II. Title.
QH105.A4B7   500.9'798   74-190658
ISBN 0-8094-1151-2
ISBN 0-8094-1153-9 lib. bdg.
ISBN 0-8094-1152-0 retail ed.

TIME-LIFE is a trademark of Time Incorporated U.S.A.

Contents

The Immensities of a Northern Wonderland

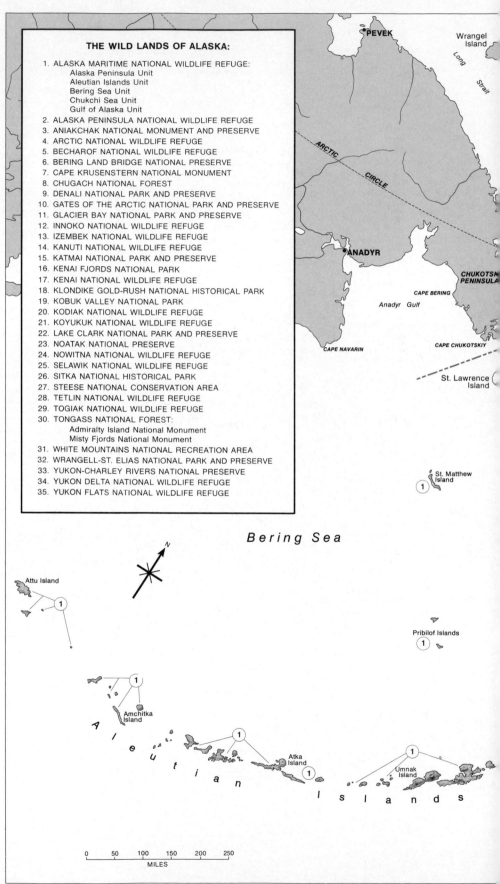

THE WILD LANDS OF ALASKA:

1. ALASKA MARITIME NATIONAL WILDLIFE REFUGE:
   Alaska Peninsula Unit
   Aleutian Islands Unit
   Bering Sea Unit
   Chukchi Sea Unit
   Gulf of Alaska Unit
2. ALASKA PENINSULA NATIONAL WILDLIFE REFUGE
3. ANIAKCHAK NATIONAL MONUMENT AND PRESERVE
4. ARCTIC NATIONAL WILDLIFE REFUGE
5. BECHAROF NATIONAL WILDLIFE REFUGE
6. BERING LAND BRIDGE NATIONAL PRESERVE
7. CAPE KRUSENSTERN NATIONAL MONUMENT
8. CHUGACH NATIONAL FOREST
9. DENALI NATIONAL PARK AND PRESERVE
10. GATES OF THE ARCTIC NATIONAL PARK AND PRESERVE
11. GLACIER BAY NATIONAL PARK AND PRESERVE
12. INNOKO NATIONAL WILDLIFE REFUGE
13. IZEMBEK NATIONAL WILDLIFE REFUGE
14. KANUTI NATIONAL WILDLIFE REFUGE
15. KATMAI NATIONAL PARK AND PRESERVE
16. KENAI FJORDS NATIONAL PARK
17. KENAI NATIONAL WILDLIFE REFUGE
18. KLONDIKE GOLD-RUSH NATIONAL HISTORICAL PARK
19. KOBUK VALLEY NATIONAL PARK
20. KODIAK NATIONAL WILDLIFE REFUGE
21. KOYUKUK NATIONAL WILDLIFE REFUGE
22. LAKE CLARK NATIONAL PARK AND PRESERVE
23. NOATAK NATIONAL PRESERVE
24. NOWITNA NATIONAL WILDLIFE REFUGE
25. SELAWIK NATIONAL WILDLIFE REFUGE
26. SITKA NATIONAL HISTORICAL PARK
27. STEESE NATIONAL CONSERVATION AREA
28. TETLIN NATIONAL WILDLIFE REFUGE
29. TOGIAK NATIONAL WILDLIFE REFUGE
30. TONGASS NATIONAL FOREST:
    Admiralty Island National Monument
    Misty Fjords National Monument
31. WHITE MOUNTAINS NATIONAL RECREATION AREA
32. WRANGELL-ST. ELIAS NATIONAL PARK AND PRESERVE
33. YUKON-CHARLEY RIVERS NATIONAL PRESERVE
34. YUKON DELTA NATIONAL WILDLIFE REFUGE
35. YUKON FLATS NATIONAL WILDLIFE REFUGE

The sizable portion of the earth's surface covered by the vast reaches of Alaska (shaded area above) is shown in detail in the map at right, which highlights the 35 federally-protected areas that cover 40 per cent of the state's 590,000 square miles.

These protected areas, whose combined size is larger than France, are identified by numbers keyed to the box at right. Included is the unique Alaska Maritime National Wildlife Refuge, whose five geographical units contain stretches of mainland coastline and many remote islands scattered over thousands of miles. The map's lettered boxes enclose four representative areas, which are the focus of this book. Detailed maps of these areas accompany the chapters describing them: A, Glacier Bay National Park and Preserve, page 43; B, Katmai National Park and Preserve, page 81; C, Denali National Park and Preserve, page 111; D, Arctic National Wildlife Refuge, page 143.

Arctic Ocean

Chukchi Sea

Banks Island

Amundsen Gulf

OBSERVATION POINT

BARROW
POINT BARROW

Teshekpuk Lake

Beaufort Sea

Prudhoe Bay

D
Barter Island

NORTH SLOPE

Mackenzie Bay

INUVIK

Great Bear Lake

CAPE LISBURNE

POINT HOPE

BROOKS RANGE

23

10

Noatak River

Colville River

Sagavanirktok River

Atigun River

4

ARCTIC VILLAGE

Table Mountain 5,042 Ft.

Sheenjek River

CANADA
UNITED STATES

Mackenzie River

ARCTIC CIRCLE

U. S. S. R.
UNITED STATES

CAPE KRUSENSTERN

7

19

Kobuk River

25

Kotzebue Sound

4

NORMAN WELLS

CAPE DEZHNEV

6

SEWARD PENINSULA

1

PROSPECT CREEK

FORT YUKON

33

Peel River

River

YUKON TERRITORY

NORTHWEST TERRITORIES

Bering Strait

1

14

35

31

27

Kobuk River

21

Yukon River

NOME

1

1

Norton Sound

TANANA

RUBY 24

FAIRBANKS

Chena River

2

DAWSON

12

Koyukuk River

Yukon River

12

C

ALASKA RANGE

KANTISHNA

9

Mt. Silverthrone 18,470 Ft.

4

2

1

28

Yukon River

Pelly River

34

McGRATH

Mt. McKinley 20,320 Ft.
Mt. Foraker 17,400 Ft.

Mt. Hunter 14,580 Ft.

32

Mt. Sanford 16,208 Ft.

WRANGELL

Mt. Blackburn 16,523 Ft.

Mt. Churchill 15,638 Ft.

ALASKA HIGHWAY

WHITEHORSE

Kuskokwim River

KUSKOKWIM MOUNTAINS

22

Susitna River

CHUGACH

4

MTS.

Copper River

Mt. Bona 16,421 Ft.

ST. ELIAS

BRITISH COLUMBIA

BETHEL

Russian Jack Springs

ANCHORAGE

17

VALDEZ

8

Sherman Glacier

MOUNTAINS

32

Mt. Saint Elias 18,008 Ft.

Mt. Vancouver 15,700 Ft.

Mt. Hubbard 14,950 Ft.

MOUNTAINS

18

Stikine River

Nunivak Island

Kuskokwim Bay

29

KENAI

1

Kenai Lake

CORDOVA

Tustumena Lake

16

SEWARD

Montague Island

1

Malaspina Glacier

Yakutat Bay
Khantaak Island

30

HAINES

A

COAST

JUNEAU

30

CAPE NEWENHAM

Iliamna Lake

B

1

Kamishak Bay

KENAI PENINSULA

1

Mt. Fairweather 15,300 Ft.

FAIRWEATHER RANGE

11

Glacier Bay

Wachusett Inlet
Bartlett Cove

PANHANDLE

PETERSBURG

Naknek Lake

5

RANGE

15

Lituya Glacier

Lituya Bay

Bristol Bay

Novarupta 3,200 Ft.

Valley of Ten Thousand Smokes

Mt. Katmai 6,715 Ft.

20

Gulf of Alaska

Admiralty Island

26

SITKA

30

WRANGELL

1

Becharof Lake

ALEUTIAN

20

KODIAK
Kodiak Island

Mist Fjords

1

1

13

ALASKA PENINSULA

2

3

1

KETCHIKAN

FORT RANDALL

2

1

Pacific Ocean

Queen Charlotte Islands

1/ The Alaskan Experience

The scenery of Alaska is so much grander than anything else of the kind in the world that, once beheld, all other scenery becomes flat and insipid.

HENRY GANNETT, 1899/ *CHIEF GEOGRAPHER, UNITED STATES GEOLOGICAL SURVEY*

You need not go far in Alaska to see moose. Flying low over the green countryside in a small plane—a favored means of transportation in a state where roads are few and distances great—you spot them standing among birches and aspens or feeding on aquatic plants in ponds and lakes. Driving, you may be startled to have one leap out of a grove of spruce on the side of the road, trot across in front of your car and disappear into the trees on the other side. In winter moose are unavoidable. They come down from the hills and mountains in search of shelter and the 15 to 25 pounds of willow, birch and aspen twigs that they must have each day to stay alive. A few come right into Alaska's towns and cities and are teased by children, chased by dogs and hit by automobiles. An average of 50 moose/car collisions occur annually in the Anchorage area alone. Along the 363 miles of railroad track between Anchorage and Fairbanks, as many as 300 moose a year have been struck by the locomotives of the Alaska Railroad, which are affectionately called "Moose Goosers" by Alaskans. (The moose carcasses are dressed and butchered, and the meat is given to charitable institutions.)

Moose are among Alaska's most spectacular animals. There are perhaps 145,000 of them in the state. Their numbers reflect, in part, a peculiarity of their Alaskan environment. The destruction of many thousands of acres of spruce forest by natural and man-caused forest fires has been a boon to moose, for among the first woody plants to spring up in such devastated areas are the willow, birch and aspen on which these herbivores browse both summer and winter. The moose have also benefited from a change in Alaska's climate. With a slight warming of the state over the years, willows have spread northward and westward into areas where formerly such shrubs grew either sparsely or not at all, and the moose have followed.

Coming upon a moose out in the wilds can be quite an experience. The Alaskan subspecies *(Alces alces gigas)* is the world's biggest moose and the largest member of the deer family. A full-grown bull may stand seven feet tall at the shoulder, weigh up to 1,800 pounds and carry 50-pound antlers measuring some 80 inches across. But once you get over your astonishment at the animal's sheer size, your inclination may be to laugh—for *Alces alces gigas* is a ridiculous-looking creature. It has jackass ears, a punching-bag nose, an overhanging muzzle, a bell, or dewlap, that dangles from its throat, a thick neck, rough brown to blackish fur, humped shoulders, a short body, long legs and a tiny rump on which a three-and-a-half-inch tail seems pinned by mistake.

The joke, however, is definitely not on the moose. Every seemingly ill-matched part has its function. Its drooping nose is keenly sensitive and so are its ears, providing an excellent early warning system should either of its enemies, the wolf or the bear, come anywhere near. The moose's long legs give it great speed and mobility. It can trot at 35 miles an hour, move easily over rough terrain and pick its way through deep snow. It uses its legs to fight back fiercely when attacked; the sharp front hooves can inflict fatal wounds. The length of the legs puts the moose at an advantage when feeding. Standing so tall, it can reach for twigs and leaves eight to nine feet above the ground; when these are beyond reach it will often rear up and straddle pliant young trees with its front legs and ride them down, thus bringing the tender shoots within range of its muzzle. The moose's rough coat also serves it well; when temperatures plunge below zero, it is one of the few animals still able to roam about in quest of food, insulated against the cold by the thick, hollow hairs that cover it.

Alaska's far-ranging moose herds are highly visible reminders of the enormousness of the wilderness here. In a state more than twice the size of Texas, but with fewer than 500,000 human inhabitants, the wilderness is often no farther away than the backyard. It stretches across four time zones and embraces distances that would reach from coast to coast and from border to border in what Alaskans call the "lower 48." It incorporates almost all of the state's three million lakes, 34,000 miles of shoreline, 10,000 rivers and streams and the 14 highest peaks in the United States, topped by 20,320-foot Mount McKinley.

About a third of Alaska's 586,000 square miles have been set aside as national parks, preserves, wildlife refuges and forests. This includes 35 designated wilderness areas that total 125,000 square miles—more than twice the size of Florida—where hunting, trapping and commercial development are either prohibited or severely restricted. Within these huge enclaves can be found barren islands and lush forests, snow-capped mountains and collapsed volcanoes, sparkling lakes and gigantic glaciers.

"For one Yosemite of California," wrote Henry Gannett at the turn of the century, "Alaska has hundreds." Indeed, 15 Yosemites could fit inside the 18,750-square-mile expanse of Alaska's Wrangell-St. Elias National Park and Preserve, the largest in the United States. But Alaska's wilderness consists of more than prodigious parklands. It contains many animals that either have vanished from the rest of the United States or are in serious decline there. Here still roam wolves—perhaps as many as 15,000. They are the north's supreme predators, feeding on plant eaters as small as the mouselike vole and as big as the moose. Here too, in large numbers, are black bears and enormous brown bears and grizzlies. And then there are the mammals not found elsewhere in the states, such as the rare musk ox, a shaggy survivor of the Great Ice Age, and the barren ground caribou, which is anything but rare: 275,000 of them roam interior and northern Alaska. Each year one and a quarter million Pacific fur seals return to the Pribilof Islands in the Bering Sea to breed and give birth to young. More than 250,000 walruses wallow in waters off the northern and western coasts. Approximately 5,500 polar bears range across the ice of the polar region. And high in the twin mountain belts of the Brooks and Alaska Ranges live some 45,000 white, curly-horned Dall sheep.

Yet in spite of so seemingly varied an animal population, Alaska does not teem with many kinds of wildlife, nor is its vegetation one of endless diversity. It has, all told, about 50 native species of land mammals, and only half as many kinds of trees as most other states. The harsh climate of much of Alaska has limited the sorts of animals and plants that can live this far north, and has required the specialization of those that can and do in order to ensure their survival. Such natural economy distinguishes the Alaskan wilderness and makes it possible to see the interrelationships of living things more easily than in lusher landscapes. In

Alaska, the threads in the web of life can often be examined one by one.

This alone would suffice to set the Alaskan wilderness apart; but there is more, much more, to stamp it as unique among America's wild areas. It is a land where nature appears at its most spectacular—and its most improbable. Things that are commonplace elsewhere seem here to be touched with a glorious madness; the real becomes surrealistic fantasy. There are trees that grow at patently absurd angles; rocks that arrange themselves in circles; mounds of earth that form strange cone shapes thousands of feet in diameter; huge ice wedges that weave intricate geometric patterns. In its angrier moods, nature in Alaska puts on performances that defy human belief. Earthquakes toss glaciers into the air, lift sea beds, denude mountains of all greenery.

The impression of great power exuded by the Alaskan wilderness is reinforced by its vastness. To speak of a single wilderness is inadequate. There are, in fact, several Alaskan wildernesses, each with its own distinctive look, from the wet and densely forested areas of the southeast to the most desolate of arctic tundra country in the far north. They vary as much as they do because Alaska is big enough to encompass several climates. These are created largely by Alaska's topography; the state is divided by three imposing mountain systems.

The first of these mountain barriers, some 1,200 miles long, consists of the Coast Mountains. In Alaska this system starts in the so-called Panhandle, that narrow strip of the state reaching southeastward along the Pacific, and then curves northwestward toward Anchorage, Alaska's largest city. The second mountain barrier, much of it impassable, is the great Alaska Range, which includes towering Mount McKinley. It runs in a 400-mile crescent from the Coast Mountains west to the Alaska Peninsula, where it joins the Aleutian Range. The third mountain barrier is the Brooks Range. While not as high as the Alaska Range, it is 150 miles wide and 600 miles long, an enormous expanse of bleak shoulders of rock. It effectively divides Alaska's interior from its northernmost sector, called the North Slope.

These different mountain systems help create very different climates. In the Panhandle, which is close to the waters warmed by the nearby Japan Current, the flow of warm, humid air moving inland from the current is intercepted by the coastal mountains rising directly from the sea. As the air ascends the western slopes and reaches cooler elevations, its moisture turns to rain and snow. Parts of the Panhandle receive 150 inches or more of precipitation a year—almost twice as much as drenches the lush rain forest of the Amazon. Juneau, Alaska's capital,

A hulking bull moose, his growing antlers covered with soft skin called velvet, browses in a clump of willow and dwarf birch. In autumn, when the antlers reach their full spread of more than six feet, the velvet will peel away and the bull will use his gleaming crown as a weapon to duel other bulls during the mating season. Then the antlers will be shed.

located about midpoint on the Panhandle, gets 55 inches annually, about 50 per cent more than proverbially damp Seattle receives. The moist, relatively mild climate produced by the liberal precipitation that falls on the Panhandle and by the Japan Current's moderating effect on air temperature, encourages plant growth. Thick groves of bristly Sitka spruce and stately Western hemlock abound. The heavy snow also feeds the glaciers that have formed in the heights of the coastal mountains and flow down through its valleys. One glacier, the Malaspina in Wrangell-St. Elias National Park and Preserve, is bigger than Rhode Island.

Similar climatic conditions prevail south of the Alaska Range. Within its protective curve the weather is mild by Alaskan standards, moderated in part by the Japan Current. Precipitation is high, 100 inches a year in some places. Sitka spruce and Western hemlock grow in the wetter eastern section, while columnar white spruce and such deciduous trees as birch, aspen and poplar thrive farther west.

Adjoining the Alaska Range, the Aleutian Range stretches 1,600 miles along the Alaskan Peninsula and beyond, where the peaks of submerged mountains form the chain of the Aleutian Islands. This range includes 80 volcanoes—about 50 of which have been active since Alaska's former owners, the Russians, began keeping track of such phenomena as eruptions—but the mountains are low-lying, and so offer little protection either to the peninsula or to the islands. Both lie in a natural storm track of the North Pacific, which exposes them to fierce gales. The Aleutian Islands, which enjoy only 36 clear days a year and are soggy, fog-shrouded and windy, are barren except for such plants as grasses and low-lying shrubs.

North of the wall formed by the Alaska and Aleutian Ranges lies Alaska's vast interior, a region of plateaus, hills and ridges through which the mighty Yukon and Kuskokwim Rivers flow. The mountains cut off much of the rain and snow that normally would move inland from the sea, and the annual precipitation varies from 20 inches down to 12. The climate is not only drier but, because of the lack of the sea's warming influence, colder. Winters, indeed, are ferociously cold. From November through March in the city of Fairbanks, which sits at the heart of the interior, the thermometer often dips to −50° F. The stands of skinny black and white spruce, birch, aspen and poplar are often scattered and broken; the unforested areas consist of tundra—a word of Finnish origin meaning land without trees—and are covered by lichens, mosses, grasses, small flowering plants and such shrubs as willow and dwarf

birch. But surprisingly, some of Alaska's highest summer temperatures and lushest vegetation can be found in the river valleys of the interior. In these valleys, called solar basins, protective rings of mountains or hills block out winds and clouds so that the valleys are bathed in almost continuous summer sunshine. Temperatures often nudge into the 90s, and the swollen rivers overflow to cover their flood plains with water warmed to about 75° F. The result is a bountiful growth of aquatic vegetation that attracts not only millions of waterfowl but sizable populations of such aquatic mammals as beaver, muskrat, mink and marten.

At the northern edge of the sprawling interior rise the rugged peaks of the Brooks Range. Stretching from the Canadian border on the east to the Chuckchi Sea on the west, this mountain system constitutes a bleak region of its own. The little moisture that still remains in the air after its passage north across the interior condenses out here as a meager eight to 12 inches of precipitation a year. As a result, plant growth is sparse. Though small stands of white spruce and other trees gain a foothold in some sheltered valleys, the slopes are generally bare except for a thin layer of hardy tundra vegetation. On the other side of the Brooks Range lies the North Slope, a vast lake-dotted plain that was once below the sea. Despite the presence of lakes and ponds and the generally marshy nature of the area in summer, it is technically a desert, for it receives only four to five inches of precipitation a year. What keeps it from being a dry desert is a layer of permafrost—permanently frozen ground—a few inches below the surface; the water cannot drain through this layer. The plain is covered with a variety of tundra plants, including dwarf willows that hug the earth to avoid the wind. During February, the coldest month, the temperature can drop to −24° F. or lower, but the average winter temperature on the North Slope is warmer than that of the interior. This is because the Arctic Ocean, like the Japan Current to the south, has a modifying maritime influence on the cold.

With all their state's diversity, it is small wonder that Alaskans refer to it as the Great Land, and to their way of life as the Alaskan Experience. And indeed they do have a unique existence. Its wellspring is nature, its driving force adventure. More than one person has come to Alaska to recharge his soul. More than one has left fulfilled, refreshed by all that he saw and did. For the nature of Alaska is such that the visitor, however casual, cannot help but respond to it. Summer days are extremely long—in some parts of the state a twilight between sunset and sunrise is all there is of night. Above the Arctic Circle at the Arctic National Wildlife Refuge the sun does not go down between May 10 and August 2, but instead circles the horizon. The radiance it sheds is of extraordinary richness, soft, yet bright; it defines objects, bringing out their beauties and colors without overwhelming them. In a land where rainbows shine at midnight, the visitor has options unavailable in the other 49 states. He can see the glaciers drop chunks of ice the size of a house into the blue-green water at Glacier Bay National Park. He can trek across the ash-filled Valley of Ten Thousand Smokes at Katmai National Park and Preserve and peer into a crater filled with steam. He can fish in a virgin pool and drink from a hundred crystal streams at the Arctic National Wildlife Refuge. He can fly above the clouds and touch down in a ski plane on the glaciers of Mount McKinley's southern slopes. He can watch the giant Alaska brown bear fish for salmon at Kamishak Bay in southwestern Alaska. In winter he can stand on the frozen Arctic Ocean and hear the ice creak and groan at the top of the world.

He can, in short, take in wild Alaska in respresentative samples—and as it happens this is not just the best way but the only way to appreciate its size and diversity. This was my own approach, and my choice of a way to start was to go dog-sledding in Denali National Park and Preserve one March weekend.

Nine furry Malamute dogs stood impatiently in the traces, barking their eagerness to get started, while at least a dozen others howled in disappointment at not getting the chance to go. Park Ranger Roy Sanborn, their trainer, an ex-Vermonter in love with northern dogs and Alaska, lashed down the load and told me to sit on top of it. Then, mounting the runners behind me, he gave the command *Hi!* The dogs strained in their harnesses, and we shot down the road and out onto the trail, heading for a log cabin on the Upper Savage River, 10 miles north of park headquarters. We were off on one of the winter patrols the rangers make to check on the wildlife.

The world lay white and silent around us. The only color, if color it can be called, was the green-black of the snow-laden spruces, and soon we had sped beyond them and out onto the tundra. The dogs were exuberant: they bit the snow, they sniffed animal smells, they dodged at the black moose droppings scattered on the trail. At the sound of their panting and the creak of the sled runners, 50 or more willow ptarmigan in white winter plumage fluttered up to our left, like an explosion of snow, and off to the right a porcupine trundled away.

Sledding by dog team is a beautiful way to travel. It is swift and natural. No barrier of metal or glass gets between you and the landscape. The cold stings the cheeks, and crumbs of ice form around the nostrils. Yet instead of being discomforted by this, you are invigorated. You see better, hear better—or at least you think you do.

The key to being a good dog-sled driver, or "musher," is keeping the sled on the narrow ribbon of packed trail. This is not easy, even with the help of a first-rate lead dog to guide the way. It takes just the right amount of pressure and weight applied to the handlebars and runners to correct any slippage to the right or left. One miscalculation and the sled can tip into the deep trailside snow. Roy had no trouble; on and on we flew without mishap. Occasionally he would halt to rest the dogs and once, when they floundered into a drift, he had to run ahead to untangle the harnesses. The dogs jumped at him and gave him loving, licking kisses. He patted and hugged them, talking to them in a high-pitched, boyish voice that they seemed to understand, then knelt and gently took out from between the pads of their paws the balls of snow and ice that had formed there.

This done, Roy hopped onto the runners and started the dogs up again. We had only a mile or so to go now, and at the command *Gee!* they veered to the right and entered a small spruce forest. The trees were furred with snow that absorbed sound and submerged us in quiet. In a clearing stood the cabin, a tiny, one-room structure of peeled logs, rich brown in color, with overhanging eaves and a heavy door through which the points of nails protruded at regular intervals—a deterrent, Roy explained, to bears.

After unharnessing the dogs and hitching them to a chain strung between two spruces, we built fires in the two wood-burning stoves and began to unload the sled. A Canada jay, a fluffy dumpling of a bird, came to watch. When we went inside, it hopped onto the crossbar of the sled and sat there, waiting, apparently, for us to drop a scrap of food. For its boldness, the species is called the camp robber.

Warmed by cups of hot black coffee brewed from melted snow, we decided to go for a hike before the early darkness of the subarctic evening closed in. In the woods animal tracks were everywhere—big ones, medium-sized ones, little ones. Foxes, snowshoe hares, porcupines, red squirrels had all passed by, yet as is so often the case where animals abound, not one was to be seen. We tramped along the trail and out onto the tundra. The wind-driven cold was now razor sharp, and we sought refuge from it inside the warm hollow of our fur-trimmed hoods.

We had not gone far when Roy spotted a moose feeding on a riverbank. Drawing closer to the thicket in which it stood, we saw that there were in fact three moose among the willows, a cow and her calf, and perhaps a bull, difficult to tell from a female because the male sheds its antlers in late fall. Where the snow had been blown off the Savage River the ice gleamed hard. Except for the spindly willows, there was nothing to shield us from the wind. We called out to the moose but our voices went skipping up into the sky. We shouted again, and this time they heard us. They trotted farther down the bank, then stopped to resume their feeding. They were obviously hungry, very hungry. The winter had been severe, and the frayed ends of willow branches, poking up through the snow like so much loose wiring at our feet, gave evidence of the animals' need. The branches had been nibbled almost to the snow line.

No longer able to take the cold, Roy and I hurried back to the cabin. Our boots crunched hollowly on the marble-white snow, and the tundra seemed more void of life than ever. On our way back the only sign of an animal was a single pawprint, raised in relief, like a fossil, the wind having chiseled away the looser snow around it. "Wolf," said Roy. Whether there was a den nearby he did not know, but he did say that more than 50 wolves lived in the park and helped keep the caribou, moose and Dall sheep healthy and their numbers under control by culling the weak and infirm from the herds.

By the time we got to the cabin, twilight had settled into the clearing, bluing the snow and darkening the trees. There were chores to be done —feeding the dogs, stoking the fires, melting snow with which to cook and wash. Roy lit the gas lantern and hung it on the pipe connecting the stoves, and then prepared two buckets of chow for his huskies, which were also to get a dried salmon apiece. The room quickly filled with the deep scent of resin from the burning spruce logs—and with so much heat that we had to leave the door ajar to let in a little cold air.

Once the dogs were fed, we had time to take care of our own needs. Roy mixed a park rangers' special, a drink called Russian tea, made with instant tea, instant lemonade, instant orange drink, water and Scotch. In the city it would have tasted vile; here in the wilderness it was delicious and made us ravenous. Soon we were seated at a rickety table, feasting on moose steaks fried in butter, canned peas and mashed potatoes. The meat was tender and juicy, rather like beef, but with a wild taste of its own. For dessert there was fruit salad, with some Russian tea poured over it.

After supper we sat and talked. The dogs had fallen asleep curled up in the snow. Darkness pressed in through the windowpanes and the lantern purred. Roy told how a couple of weeks earlier wolves had gathered near another cabin he used on his rounds and howled through most of the night. "They meant no harm," he said. "They'd picked up the scent of the female dogs and just wanted to be near them." This appreciation of wolves pleased me. They have been too long the victims of the Red Ridinghood myth that portrays them as gobblers of grannies and children, when in fact they are quite timid around humans. In all of North America there has been only one documented instance of a wolf attacking a man.

We stopped talking and listened for some sound outside; there was none. If wolves were in the vicinity, they kept the secret to themselves. We grew drowsy in the warmth. Though it was not yet 9 o'clock, getting to bed was a welcome prospect. Following Roy's example, I took a caribou skin that we had brought with us, spread it on my bunk for insulation, then put my sleeping bag on top of it. When I woke the next morning, the fires were out, but only my face was cold.

The trip by dog sled, the excitement of being where the animals live, the beauty of the land—all added up to an adventure of peculiarly Alaskan dimensions. Even the contact with the intense and potentially deadly cold, felt most while we watched the hungry moose feed on the ragged willows, enhanced the excitement. The sense of how vulnerable a human is in a land this huge and harsh puts an edge on all Alaskan wilderness experiences. Nature is still a threat here—and not just out in the wilds, but in the cities as well. Juneau fears avalanches from the mountains that tower behind it. Fairbanks, which is on a swift, narrow river, the Chena, worries about floods that melting snows or even summer rains may bring. Anchorage, scene of one of the most violent earthquakes on record, wonders when the next great shock will occur. And almost everywhere in the state there is concern about the cold (Alaska's lowest recorded temperature, −79.8° F., was set on January 23, 1971, at Prospect Creek, which is located just north of the Arctic Circle).

The true Alaskan, the sourdough, is someone who has experienced several seasons of cold, snow and darkness, kept a hold on his nerves and survived. To draw water, he may have to dangle a hot poker down a frozen pipe, and his idea of hell may be a visit to his outhouse in sub-zero weather. Yet ask him if he likes winter and you may be surprised by his answer. Often he will reply that he loves it. And why not? The winter has its own beauty—the moonlit darkness, the silver snow, the star-

A pair of 19th Century visitors to Alaska's Glacier Bay gaze downward on the sprawling mass of Muir Glacier 1,800 feet below.

pierced sky, the sheets and curtains of green and red light in the ionosphere that flash the message of the aurora borealis. And, of course, there is the fundamental challenge of survival.

No living thing can survive here that is not adapted to, or equipped for, the cold. In Jack London's famous story, "To Build a Fire," a cheechako, the sourdoughs' word for tenderfoot, sets out in early morning —alone except for a dog—to join his friends camped a day's hike away. He does not realize how really cold it is—a deception possible in those parts of the north where the air is bone dry—but when he spits, the saliva crackles as it falls to the ground. He trudges on. His cheeks and the end of his nose ache; his moist breath quickly powders his mustache, eyebrows and eyelashes with frost. For one brief moment he exposes his fingers to the cold and is "astonished at the swift numbness that smote them." The sting that touches his toes gradually passes, and he wonders whether they are warm or numb.

Then, when he least expects it, he breaks through the ice and gets soaked to his knees. His moccasins freeze; his socks turn into "sheaths of iron." He knows that he must start a fire to prevent his feet from being frostbitten, but his first attempt fails when the flames are doused by snow cascading from the branches of a spruce. Already he has lost the function of his hands. Only by extreme effort can he open his mouth, now nearly frozen shut, and grasp a match between his teeth. He manages to strike it but the fumes spurt up his nostrils, making him cough —and the match goes out. In desperation he manages to manipulate the whole bunch of matches between the heels of his hands and scratch them on his leg. As 70 sulphur matches light at once his flesh starts to burn, yet he feels at first only the mildest of sensations. In his clumsy efforts to feed the fire he extinguishes it.

Now he knows that it is no longer "a mere matter of freezing his fingers and toes, or of losing his hands and feet, but . . . a matter of life and death with the chances against him." He is thrown into panic. Frantically he begins to run. He stumbles repeatedly, and finally falls down. The snow is warm. The first waves of drowsiness come. As his blood and flesh congeal, he dreams of his friends finding his body. The dog approaches, sniffs his inert form and retreats. The man is dead.

Nearly a century after London wrote, winter remains the single most crucial fact of life in Alaska. In the interior it may last nine months or longer. The Bering Sea is packed with ice from November until the last days of June; on the North Slope, the sun disappears in mid-November and does not reappear until the last days of January. Winter produces the snow that feeds the state's 28,000 square miles of glaciers. It causes the massive freeze-ups that turn mighty rivers like the Yukon into ice-paved highways and that lead, come spring, to the massive breakups. Bets are taken as to just when the ice will go out in a particular river. And when it does—in April, May or June—it is something never to forget. The water builds up over the ice, and at the same time the ice rises. A creaking and groaning are heard, and then with a roar, followed by a crunching and rumbling, the ice tears loose.

One old-timer recalled watching his first breakup years ago at Fairbanks, where the narrow Chena flows through town. "As far as could be seen upriver was a never-ending procession of ice floes," he said, "grinding and swirling; turning up on edge and sticking up for a dozen feet or more." The floes tore into a barge and a boat and splintered them, snapped off a bridge built on piles "and the bridge itself mounted a floe and rode away." Downstream, the ice undermined a warehouse and carried it around a bend and out of sight, contents and all. There was still more the old-timer remembered seeing go by: huge trees, tin cans from cabins upstream, dead dogs, live rabbits stranded on the ice when the run started.

Even with the coming of summer and the long days of endless sunlight, the cold keeps a grip on most of Alaska. All but the southern coastal area has a mean annual temperature below freezing; thus the air often has bite, and it is air you do not just breathe, but feel on the skin. It colors the cheeks, stiffens the fingers a little. Snow may fall in June and autumn arrives in August. Aspens and willows turn yellow, and the leaves of dwarf birch and blueberry flame red. Dig into the earth at any time during the summer, and in many places you will find the ground frozen a foot or so down. Fully 85 per cent of the state is underlaid by permafrost—soil, gravel or rock that has remained at a temperature below 32° F. for two years or more. At the Eskimo community of Barrow on the North Slope the permafrost is 1,300 feet thick and several thousand years old.

This permanently frozen ground greatly affects the character of the Alaskan wildernesses, seriously impeding drainage and determining to a large extent the pattern of the vegetation. Around Fairbanks, for example, white spruce, birch, cottonwood and certain willows thrive where the permafrost is four feet or more below the surface and allows sufficient room for their roots. Black spruces, with their shallow root systems, can survive where the frozen layer is less than four feet down, but even they are unable to grow where the permafrost lies within the top 18 inches or so. Low alder, dwarf birch, aromatic Labrador tea, blueberry, wild cranberry, moss and lichens grow where the layer of unfrozen soil is thin. From the air, it is surprising to see how much of Alaska is treeless land of this type.

From the air something else may become apparent—the wonderfully surrealistic quality of much of the landscape. There is, to begin with, a peculiar cracked patterning of the ground, rather like sun-baked mud in appearance, and most conspicuous in the northern half of the state. This too is a manifestation of winter and is associated with permafrost. Scientists believe it comes about in the following manner. The topmost layer of ground thaws in the summer. The onset of cold causes the thawed ground to freeze and contract—sometimes with a loud bang —and a network of cracks to form. In the early spring water trickles into these cracks; during the still-frigid nights it freezes. Meanwhile the slowly thawing ground above the permafrost expands, closing the cracks and sealing in the ice. Winter returns and the cracks reopen; spring pours more water in—and as the process is repeated year after year the ice increases gradually in size and becomes a vertical wedge from a quarter of an inch to 10 feet thick and from four to 30 feet deep. Seen from the air, the ice wedges often show up as interconnected depressions in the surface. They may form triangular, square, rectangular and even round patterns; scientists refer to such ice-patterned land as polygonal, or many-angled, ground.

A thin layer of insulating vegetation covers and preserves these ice wedges. If it is removed—by a bulldozer, for example—the heat of the sun melts the underlying ice, and as it subsides deep pits may form, the walls of which collapse when the permafrost thaws in summer. These pits fill with water to become ponds and eventually small lakes.

Winter leaves its mark on the Alaskan wildernesses in other strikingly visible ways. Stones will often be found lying in circles called nets. Nets form when the ground freezes and contracts into mounds, squeezing rocks to the surface as it does so. The larger rocks then slide down the sloping sides of the mounds to form encircling rings. Many such rings may join in a network, like a series of tiny walled gardens. When frost heaving occurs on gentle slopes, the larger stones may roll downhill, where they gather in looping garlands. On steeper slopes they lie in parallel rows that point downhill.

Even more dramatic are pingos, mounds that form when water is trapped between the permafrost, which inhibits drainage, and the surface of the ground. As this water freezes, it expands and heaves the ground upward, making a conical hill of soil and ice. Pingos can be thousands of feet in diameter and more than 100 feet high. Often they have water-filled craters on top, where the ice—after causing the pingo to form—has melted and produced a partial cave-in.

In another example of frost action, seasonal thawing of the ground on moisture-saturated slopes may cause the soil to slide slowly down over the permafrost and carry the vegetation with it. Trees so transported lose their balance and seem to be staggering off in several directions at once. In Denali park one such erratic stand of white spruce goes by the name of Drunken Forest.

Besides modifying the land in many different ways, frost action sculpts Alaska's mountain chains, splitting and shattering the rock and sending great chunks tumbling down the slopes. Bob Marshall, who explored the Brooks Range during the 1930s, had vivid evidence of this. He tells in his *Alaska Wilderness* of climbing a ridge and hearing a loud noise like an explosion above him. He looked up "to see a big rock, probably six feet across, plunging down the mountainside in my general direction. I started to run, but slipped and sprawled flat. When I looked again, it seemed to be coming straight for me and it was too late to move. . . . I lay just as flat as I could, knowing that chunks like this, bounding down the mountainside, hit the ground only now and then. Fortunately the spot where I was lying was neither now nor then, so I was soon on my way once more, a bit shakily, to the top of the ridge."

When Marshall reached the top, he realized that he had achieved a much-dreamed-of goal. He was standing on the Arctic Divide, the dividing line between two great drainage systems—on one side all the streams and rivers flowed northward into the Arctic Ocean, on the other south into the Yukon and its tributaries or west into Kotzebue Sound. And before him unfolded the most impressive view he had ever seen: 10 ridges, each of a knife-edge sharpness caused by glacial erosion, each faced with a giant precipice and each soaring two to three thousand feet from the valley floor.

Marshall's close call was only one of several he had while exploring the Brooks Range, but he was not a man to turn back. He allowed himself to be forever drawn forward by the next unnamed valley, the next unscaled mountain. He was responding not just to Alaska's wild beauty —its outrageous magnificence, as Sigurd Olson, the writer-naturalist, has called it—but to the challenge of the land itself, to its danger. This

is what can make adventuring in Alaska such a profound experience; there are forces at work here so much bigger than man, whether they be a six-foot rock bounding toward you—or an earthquake.

Southern Alaska and the Aleutian Islands lie along one of the world's most active seismic zones. On several occasions during this century the area has been rocked by severe earthquakes. During one period of particularly violent activity in 1912 a new volcano, appropriately named Novarupta, blew up with an earth-shattering explosion. Shortly thereafter, an older neighboring volcano, Mount Katmai, collapsed as the lava beneath it drained away. In the short space of 60 hours, seven cubic miles of pumice and ash were hurled toward the sky from Novarupta. For three days the ash settled over a 42,000-square-mile area. On Kodiak Island, 100 miles to the southeast of the Alaska Peninsula, the inhabitants groped in the darkness, convinced that the world was coming to an end. Today, the site of the 1912 eruption forms part of the 6,550-square-mile Katmai park.

Another powerful earthquake, which was felt in 1958 throughout a large part of southeastern Alaska, had quite different effects. It struck at 10:17 p.m. during one of Alaska's long evenings of summer twilight. Two couples from Yakutat, together with a woman friend, had been picking wild strawberries on Khantaak Island, located in Yakutat Bay—some three miles north of their hometown and 200 miles northwest of Juneau. One of the couples had started off for home in their boat and the other three people were preparing to board theirs when the earth heaved and the southern portion of the island on which the trio were standing suddenly rose 20 feet—and then just as suddenly plunged 200 feet into the bay. They were never seen again. Some 135 miles to the southeast a fisherman and his wife watched the coast from the deck of their boat "as a whole mountain came down." The wife later reported, "It felt like our boat jumped 12 feet out of the water. The dust and smoke from the mountain lasted for hours."

The 1958 earthquake inflicted its greatest devastation on Lituya Bay, 125 miles northwest of Juneau. This T-shaped inlet, measuring approximately six and a half miles in length and two miles across at its widest point, has a narrow entrance where a spit juts from the shore. Behind Lituya Bay rise some of the snowy peaks of the Fairweather Range, and at this point three glaciers feed into the bay.

That evening three fishing boats had cast anchor in the bay's calm waters. At the moment the quake struck one of the fishermen looked up to

Moving seaward past peaks more than a mile high, Rainbow Glacier becomes a gigantic icefall on its way to a fjord in Southeast Alaska.

behold an incredible sight. "The mountains were shaking something awful with slides of rock and snow," he reported, "but what I noticed mostly was the glacier, the north glacier, the one they call Lituya Glacier. I know you can't ordinarily see that glacier from where I was anchored. But I know what I saw. The glacier had risen in the air and moved forward so it was in sight. It must have risen several hundred feet. It was shaking like crazy. Big chunks of ice were falling off the face. And then suddenly the glacier dropped back out of sight."

What happened next was even harder to believe. A giant wave, perhaps 100 feet high, raced down the bay. The fisherman felt his boat rise on it. "We went away up over the trees," he said, "and I looked down on rocks as big as an ordinary house as we crossed the spit. We were way up above them. It felt like we were in a tin can and somebody was shaking it." Deposited on the other side of the spit, the boat soon sank, but the fisherman and his wife were able to escape in a punt. Another less fortunate couple went right to the bottom with their boat. A third fisherman and his seven-year-old son also managed to ride out the wave —but they had one moment of extreme terror when they tried to raise their anchor and found that it would not budge. The vessel rode up the face of the wave, anchor chain still attached. "But no chain, not even the heavy one I use," the father recollected, "could stand that strain. As the boat began her almost perpendicular ascent to the crest of the wave, the chain snapped." And this boat too was swept to safety.

Where did this protean wave come from? Geologists think that the earthquake set loose an enormous rockslide, with an estimated volume of 40 million cubic yards, that thundered from a slope at the upper end of the bay into the deep inlet. The resulting splash surged 1,740 feet high up the spur of a mountain opposite and leaped over it, while the wave itself poured from the entrance of the inlet, bounced back and forth, then raced down the bay at a speed ranging between 97 and 130 miles an hour. By that time several smaller waves had developed, and for 25 minutes or so the water in Lituya Bay sloshed back and forth as though in a washbasin. When it was all over, the mountainside opposite the original rockslide had been denuded to bedrock; four square miles of forest along both shores had been ripped out.

Six years later, in 1964, another Alaskan earthquake—the greatest ever recorded in North America—wrought havoc through the southern half of the state. It lasted for about four minutes and had a force somewhere between 8.3 and 8.75 on the Richter scale (at least as powerful as the destructive San Francisco quake of 1906, which has been estimated at 8.3). Though only 114 lives were lost in Alaska, the quake literally moved mountains, shifting some by as much as 50 feet, depressing others by almost 10 feet. The shock elevated a 275-by-75-mile portion of sea bed between Kodiak and Montague Islands as high as 50 feet and lifted 50-mile-long Montague Island, close to the center of the shock, more than 30 feet, tilting it in the process.

At the focal point of the quake, about 80 miles southeast of heavily damaged Anchorage, the violent rocking of the ground whipped the trees until their tops snapped off. At Kenai Lake, on the Kenai Peninsula, rockslides set in motion by the quake plunged into the water and produced waves so violent that they peeled the bark off tree trunks to a height of 20 feet. Near Sherman Glacier, also in southern Alaska, the summit and side of a mountain dropped off and formed a flying carpet of debris more than a mile wide and two miles long. The drooping edges of the carpet apparently confined a mass of compressed air and the rock fragments riding this displaced air, traveling at a speed of more than 115 miles an hour, flew 10,000 feet across a 450-foot-high ridge and landed on the glacial ice.

In the wake of the tremors followed a series of seismic sea waves, some of which swelled 50 to 220 feet high. They washed out sections of the cities of Kodiak, Seward and Cordova, completely destroyed four villages and damaged 10 other communities. Some of the waves rolled clear across the Pacific to Japan, and one arrived 22½ hours after the quake on the frozen shores of Antarctica, 8,445 miles away, having traveled at a speed of 430 miles an hour—a measure of the power behind only one of the forces that shape and reshape wild Alaska.

2/ A Region Reborn

At length the clouds lifted a little, and beneath their gray fringes I saw the berg-filled expanse of the bay... a solitude of ice and snow and newborn rocks, dim, dreary, mysterious.   JOHN MUIR/ TRAVELS IN ALASKA

Who has not wanted to journey back in time and see the world when it was young? In Alaska you can. Not only is much of Alaska virgin land, but there are parts of it that offer glimpses of the processes by which the earth was shaped and life took hold. One such place is Glacier Bay National Park and Preserve, located on Alaska's thickly forested southeastern coast, only 50 air miles from the state capital of Juneau. The park covers 5,289 square miles of mountainous wilderness, and is cut in two by the enormous, island-dotted bay from which it takes its name. When it is seen from the air, this 65-mile-long body of water resembles a large tree of many branches, each branch an inlet. No fewer than 16 glaciers feed into the inlets and the bay from the surrounding mountains, and they regularly unloose gigantic icebergs that then float down the waters of the bay to the sea.

But what is most remarkable about the park is not its icebergs, its awesome bay, its vast expanses of ice and snow or the grandeur of its mountains—one of them, Mount Fairweather, more than 15,000 feet high. Rather it is the fact that here one is able to see what much of the northern part of the continent must have looked like 10,000 to 15,000 years ago when the glaciers of the Great Ice Age were retreating northward and the glacier-scoured earth was awakening from its long sleep under the ice. Many of Glacier Bay's glaciers are stable or even growing. But some are slowly melting; as they melt, ground that has been covered with ice for thousands of years is exposed. At first it is totally barren. Then, slowly, vegetation begins to cover the exposed rocks and dirt. Mosses and other low-growing plants establish colonies; later, bushes and trees take over until finally the land is forested once more—as it was before the glaciers formed. Each of these basic stages of the life cycle is visible in the park.

This process—ecologists call it a plant succession—has been going on at Glacier Bay ever since a slight warming of the world's climate, starting in the 18th Century, began to melt the ice in the region. In 1794, when the British explorer George Vancouver, one of the first Europeans to sail along Alaska's southeastern coast, beheld the mouth of Glacier Bay, he found it blocked by "an immense body of compact perpendicular ice, extending from shore to shore, and connected with a range of lofty mountains on each side."

At the time, the glacier had been on the advance for some 3,000 years and extended inland for 100 miles. But by the end of the 19th Century it had receded 40 miles up the bay. Water again filled the channel the ice had clogged, and the raw, naked land along each side of the bay gradually became covered with green. Today, as the glaciers continue their retreat, the succession process still goes on in the upper reaches of the bay, offering a unique opportunity to see how land that has been long imprisoned by ice comes back to life.

My introduction to this emerging realm took place in the month of February. With one of the park's rangers, I journeyed to Riggs Glacier in the National Park Service's patrol boat. We set out from the park headquarters on Bartlett Cove—the approximate site of the towering face of the great glacier when Vancouver saw it in 1794. Riggs Glacier, although still immense, is a comparatively tiny fragment of this once overwhelming ice sheet. It lies near the head of Muir Inlet, one of Glacier Bay's numerous branches. Its distance from Bartlett Cove, 45 miles, is a measure of how strikingly the glacial ice has fallen back in the last two centuries.

The trip to Riggs Glacier was a long one, even in the speedy boat. Bucking wind and waves, we were more than half a day getting there. The morning light, such as it was, slid in under a ledge of gray sky and wanly illuminated the jagged peaks of the distant Fairweather Range. Above the stony beaches flanking the blue-green water, snow-bundled spruces stood close together. But the farther we ventured up the bay, the scarcer the spruces became, and soon wispy cottonwoods appeared.

The cottonwoods in turn thinned, and bushy alders, a relative of the birches, predominated. Then the alders disappeared and there was nothing but snow—miles and miles of snow where only recently glacial ice had covered the land.

Throughout our trip the effects of the ice were clearly visible. Many of the hills and ridges had been rounded and smoothed by it; others seemed to have been sheared off by the moving glacier; still others, rough slopes composed of piles of rock dumped by the glacier when it retreated, were garlanded with frozen waterfalls. Sheathed in snow, the low ridges left by rockslides bulged like veins in a man's arm. On some heights tall hemlocks grew, ancient survivors of the forest that covered these mountains before the glacier began its last advance 3,000 years ago. Such forested areas endured because they stood higher than the ice; those in its path were destroyed by it. The remains of trees that had been overrun by the glacier lay on the beaches. Stumps that were several millennia old protruded among the beach pebbles. They had been buried in sand and gravel by glacial streams, then covered by the ice itself, and then, as the ice receded, exhumed by tides and storms.

As the boat plowed on, the vista became ever more dismal. Land on water appeared lifeless; not a bird or animal was to be seen. Worsening weather added an ominous touch. Streamers of black and gray mist hung in horizontal layers on the mountains. Snow, rain and sleet fell intermittently; the dampness and cold crept under our clothes and settled next to the skin. Just as we had given up hope of seeing another living creature, we spotted what looked like a stump on a tiny island. Then the "stump" moved—a bald eagle. The long pliable feathers at its wing tips clutched the air like fingers and propelled the bird forward. As it soared overhead, a hair seal bobbed up in front of the boat to take one long curious look. Then both vanished, and we were alone again.

Awe—in the old-fashioned sense of fear—is a component of the more profound wilderness experiences. Where we were at the moment, the changeable, moody weather and the hulking mountains would have been enough to instill it. But confronted with a setting that would survive us, that did not care in the least about us, that was so utterly impassive, that was still in the process of becoming, like a thought not yet formed, we felt lost, overwhelmed. Our only mark was the trail of foam the boat left, and that soon disappeared.

As we approached Riggs Glacier, chunks of ice closed around us. We drifted toward the glacier through the pri- (continued on page 46)

A hint of the rugged grandeur of Glacier Bay National Park and Preserve, which is described in this chapter, appears in the intricate pattern of peaks and glaciers shown on this map. The park lies in the upper Panhandle section of southeastern Alaska (blue area in inset map). Glacier Bay itself, with its many islands and narrow inlets, snakes its way among the peaks and gray-blue ice fields. The park boundaries are outlined by solid red lines. Dotted red lines indicate the park's designated wilderness areas.

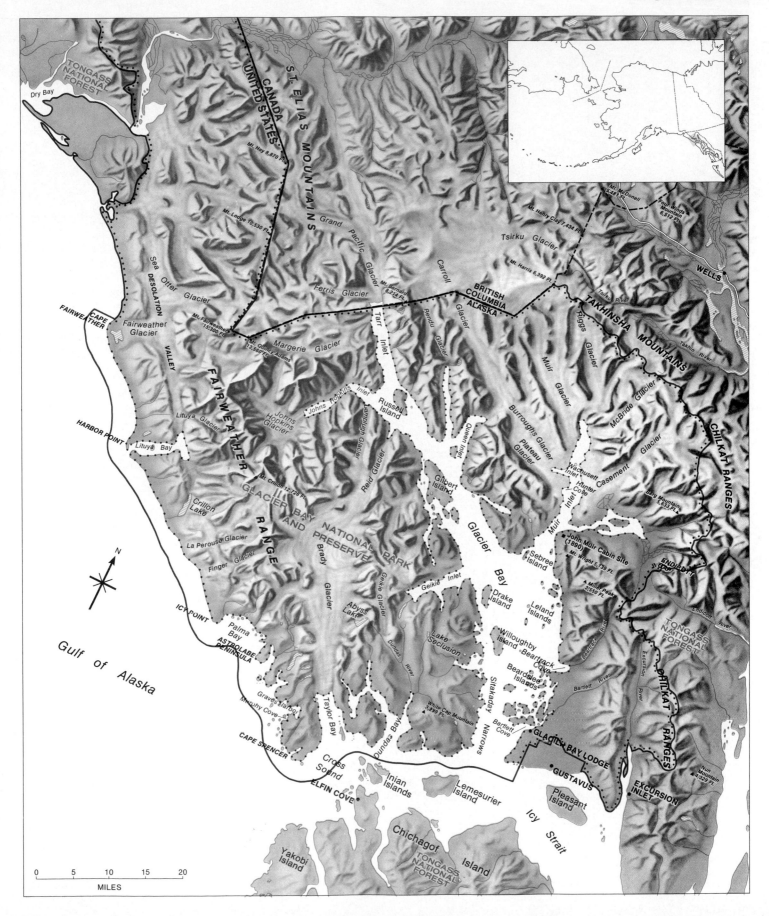

Gulf of Alaska

TONGASS NATIONAL FOREST

Dry Bay

ST. ELIAS MOUNTAINS

CANADA
UNITED STATES

Mt. Hay 8,870 Ft.

Mt. Lodge 10,530 Ft.

Grand Pacific Glacier

Ferris Glacier

Sea Otter Glacier

DESOLATION VALLEY

FAIRWEATHER

CAPE FAIRWEATHER

Fairweather Glacier

Mt. Bernard 8,244 Ft.

Mt. Fairweather 15,300 Ft.

Mt. Quincy Adams 13,560 Ft.

Margerie Glacier

Carroll

Rendu Glacier

Tarr Inlet

Reid Glacier

Lamplugh Glacier

Johns Hopkins Inlet

Russell Island

Mt. Henry Clay 7,434 Ft.

Tsirku Glacier

Mt. Harris 6,392 Ft.

BRITISH COLUMBIA
ALASKA

Glacier

Riggs Glacier

Muir Glacier

McBride Glacier

Casement Glacier

Mt. McDonell 5,491 Ft.

Four Winds Mountain 6,512 Ft.

WELLS

TAKHINSHA MOUNTAINS

Tsirku River

Takhin River

CHILKAT RANGES

HARBOR POINT

Lituya Glacier

Lituya Bay

Johns Hopkins Glacier

FAIRWEATHER RANGE

Mt. Crillon 12,726 Ft.

Crillon Lake

La Perouse Glacier

Finger Glacier

GLACIER BAY AND PRESERVE

NATIONAL PARK

Brady Glacier

Queen Inlet

Gilbert Island

Burroughs Glacier

Plateau Glacier

Wachusett Inlet

Hunter Cove

Muir Inlet

Berg Mountain 5,839 Ft.

John Muir Cabin Site (1890)

Mt. Wright 5,139 Ft.

Millar Peak 3,550 Ft.

ENDICOTT

TONGASS NATIONAL FOREST

Endicott River

ICY POINT

Palma Bay

ASTROLABE PENINSULA

Abyss Lake

Geikie Glacier

Geikie Inlet

Drake Island

Leland Islands

Sebree Island

Glacier Bay

Lake Seclusion

Willoughby Island

Beartrack Cove

Beardslee Islands

Bartlett River

Eastfield River

Excursion River

CHILKAT RANGES

Graves Harbor

Murphy Cove

Taylor Bay

Dundas River

Lake

White Cap Mountain 3,299 Ft.

Sitakaday Narrows

Bartlett Cove

GLACIER BAY LODGE

Nun Mountain 3,329 Ft.

CAPE SPENCER

Dundas Bay

Cross Sound

ELFIN COVE

Inian Islands

Lemesurier Island

GUSTAVUS

Pleasant Island

EXCURSION INLET

Icy Strait

Yakobi Island

Chichagof Island

TONGASS NATIONAL FOREST

N

MILES
0   5   10   15   20

Johns Hopkins Inlet, flanked by lofty mountains of the Fairweather Range, glimmers eerily in the weak winter-afternoon light. The head

of the inlet (background) is choked by the Johns Hopkins Glacier. The peak behind the glacier, its top hidden by clouds, is 10,000 feet high.

meval silence. The closest we could get was half a mile; we were stopped by an apron of ice. But even at this distance, the glacier was a presence. Forming a wall about 150 feet high and nearly a mile wide, it seemed more stone than ice, unreal. A section of it that rested on the beach had a muddy, mineralized look, but where the glacier extended into the inlet the wall was pearly blue. Not until I had stared for a while at the sheaves and columns of fragmented ice and peered into the cracks and crevasses through field glasses did I finally accept the reality of the glacier's huge mass. In the meantime, chunks of floating ice had crowded around the boat and were beginning to block our exit. As we pulled away, three hair seals surfaced and studied us with black, glistening eyes. They were the only other living things in sight, and we felt a kinship with them.

The next time I saw Riggs Glacier was on a sunny summer's day. I came to the glacier by a longer, more circuitous route and by a different means of transport—a small plane that was equipped with pontoons for landing on water. My pilot and I took off from the same place where I had started the winter trip, the park headquarters at Bartlett Cove. Here, Sitka spruces and Western hemlocks now flourish where the glacier reached its outermost limit 200 years ago and dumped its immense load of sand. The trees have been abetted in their growth by the 75 inches of precipitation that fall annually on the area around the cove. They are now so tall, so covered with mosses and lichens, that they seem to have been rooted on the spot forever. Here the land that was once covered by glacier has been wholly reclaimed. Toward the end of our flight we would be touching down in areas where the process of reclamation is still going on.

We flew west toward the seacoast, crossing the mouth of Glacier Bay and heading for Brady Glacier, the largest in the park. Below us were the green spires of a spruce-hemlock-cedar forest, through which snaked a turquoise river, the blue color lightened by glacial flour— finely ground particles of ice-abraded rock. Through open patches among the trees we were able to see muskegs, or bogs; here and there ponds of various sizes shimmered. Before long the Brady loomed into view, a broad, glowing band of ice three miles wide that flowed down from an enormous basin high in the mountains and terminated in a mud flat cut by braided streams carrying melt-off from the glacier. Where these streams ran across the silt into the sea, the deep blue of the ocean was lightened again to turquoise.

We came in low over a coastal inlet rimmed by hemlocks, landing at a place called Murphy Cove. Beaching the plane, the pilot and I began to explore. Behind the tall screen of trees along the shore lay a muskeg—known as one of the most beautiful bogs in the park. We reached it by climbing through a shaded ravine filled with moss-draped stones, roots and tree trunks. Where the forest thinned and the muskeg began, skunk cabbages with wide, flaring leaves grew; their strong odor blended pungently with the dank scent of the acidic bog. The giant skunk-cabbage leaves had not yet fully unfurled, but a yellow callalike flower thrust up from a stiff stalk at the center of each plant. The ground of the muskeg rose in gentle swells padded with moss, lichens and sedges. On this soft carpet bloomed pink bells of bog laurel and bog rosemary, sparkling puffs of white Labrador tea, the shirred stems of yellow lousewort and a dozen other tiny bog flowers. Around the dark pools that were scattered every few yards over the muskeg grew low, spreading mountain hemlock; Alaska, or yellow, cedar with limp feather-shaped branches; and stunted lodgepole pine, with gracefully contorted branches reminiscent of a Japanese dwarf, or bonsai, tree. Indeed, this muskeg, with its unintentionally contrived look, could almost have been a Japanese garden. As we were leaving the bog, a strong sound, as if someone were blowing across the mouth of an empty cider bottle, broke the stillness. It was the low, booming call of the blue grouse, a bird that inhabits forests and the edges of muskegs.

Making our way back to the plane, we took off again into an overcast that had rolled in from the sea. The pilot headed north along the shore looking for a hole in the clouds and soon found one. Diving through it, we flew low across a fractured landscape of crevassed ice flows and boulders and out into Lituya Bay, where the giant wave was loosed by the memorable earthquake of 1958. Years later the devastation was still evident. Straight ahead of us was the steep slope from which the rockslide had tumbled into the water. Opposite it was the rock shoulder of the mountain that had received the full brunt of the gigantic splash, and had been stripped of all vegetation to a height of 1,740 feet. All along the bay itself lay the remains of dead trees, some of them stacked in piles 20 to 30 feet high.

Again heading north, we flew over a wide sandy beach with spruces rearing behind it like a palisade, in an unwavering line miles long. A deep, dark forest spread inland, covering an area that had escaped not only the glaciation of 3,000 years ago, but also, perhaps, the even more massive ice sheet laid down during the Great Ice Age.

Here, in what scientists call a refugium, or natural asylum, plants and animals may have survived unharmed, although others nearby had been displaced or destroyed by the ice. Below us venerable hemlocks stood massed in such thick stands that only the merest glimmerings of light could possibly penetrate to the forest floor.

The timelessness of the refugium contrasted with the end-of-the-world impression given by the landscape we saw still farther north. Here various plants, including bushy alder, had managed to take root on stony rubble that had collected on top of the ice of the immense, sprawling Fairweather Glacier. The plants helped to create a thin layer of soil from which spruce and hemlock had eventually sprung up. Now the ice underneath their roots is melting, and the trees have begun to fall over as their support gives way. Some have toppled into dark, seemingly bottomless pits and others have slid down hillsides, taking the earth with them and baring the steel-gray ice beneath. This scene of weird devastation gave way farther north to one almost as eerie. Piles of dirt and rock towered everywhere, as though some superhuman construction project had suddenly been abandoned. These mounds are the product of the glacier, which in its flow has gouged chunks of rock from the mountains and left them in heaps at its farthest points of advance.

From this topsy-turvy place so close to the coast, we flew inland toward the mountains of the Fairweather Range and circled back toward Glacier Bay. The cloud cover had thinned and the sun was out. The mountain snow gleamed with a brightness that hurt the eye. On the precipitous slopes it slumped like wet plaster of paris; on less steep inclines, it was as fluffy as sifted flour, or soft and lumpy, like confectioners' sugar. And below us were the park's biggest glaciers, pouring out of amphitheaters and valleys in what seemed, from our vantage point, like the smoothest of ribbons.

Contrary to what one might expect, there are many more glaciers in the southern part of Alaska than in its far north. This fact has less to do with the temperature than with the amount of snow that falls on each region. The Brooks Range, at the edge of the Arctic Circle, gets only eight to 12 inches of precipitation a year and hence has few big glaciers. The southeastern coast, adjacent to the moisture-producing Gulf of Alaska and the Japan Current, gets a great deal more. Even in summer, warm, humid air rising into the cooler atmosphere of the mountains of this coast may yield snow. As it accumulates on the heights it turns to ice. When the ice reaches a certain density and volume it begins to flow of its own mass and weight, and a glacier is born.

But for a glacier to stay healthy, it needs frequent feedings of snow. In recent years, the glaciers lying at the higher altitudes have fared well and even grown because the snowfall has been adequate to their needs. But farther down the slopes snowfall has lessened, and many glaciers have been shrinking fast.

Riggs Glacier is not one of these and, even from high above, it was an impressive sight. We landed quite close to it, taxied up to the shore and climbed out onto the beach. What had been so hard to see clearly in the sleet and rain of winter now spread before me in a dazzling, sunlit semicircle. From within the massive blue-and-white wall of Riggs came rumblings as the cracked and crevassed ice shifted. A report like a rifle shot rang out whenever a small chunk broke off and plunged into the lagoon in front. The sound made me stiffen, but it was nothing, I thought, compared to the thunder one hears when a glacier calves. Undermined by the high tides characteristic of the park's waters, enormous blocks break off from the ice face, plummet into the water and rise, sending waves racing that can swamp or capsize a skiff—and all this happens with a roar that is as thrilling as it is frightening.

The bare land on which we stood was the prologue in the drama of plant succession. Less than a dozen years before, it had been covered by the Riggs ice. Now it was exposed, but we saw no signs of growth on the rocks and silt, not even lichens and mosses. Yet one day this patch of land will be as lush as the thickly vegetated islands we saw on our flight back to Bartlett Cove.

To observe the steps by which plants invade areas freed of ice—and then proliferate to the point where a forest comes into being—I arranged to accompany biologist Gregory Streveler, again by boat, on a trip from Bartlett Cove to Wachusett Inlet. This 10-mile fjord branches off Muir Inlet, and its rocky shores were laid bare only within this century by the retreat of Plateau Glacier, which still sprawls in a semicircle at its upper end. Because the ground at Wachusett Inlet emerged from the ice so recently, it is a good place to study the start of plant succession. Our plan was to camp on the beach near the glacier for a couple of days and examine the pioneering species that have taken hold in the muck and rubble. From there, we would make our way back to Bartlett Cove, pausing occasionally to investigate the increasingly complex communities of plants covering land freed from the glaciers' grip in the 18th and 19th Centuries. We would then spend some time in the spruce-hemlock forest at Bartlett Cove, and finally go for an af-

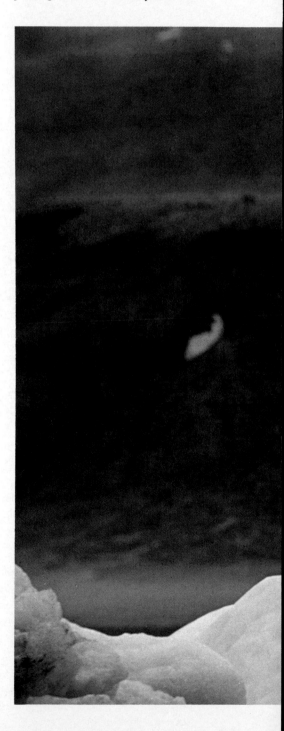

Watching intently for its fish dinner to swim by, a bald eagle hitches a ride on an iceberg calved by one of the many glaciers in Glacier Bay park. Found in large numbers in the area, this noble-looking bird does not grow its familiar white head and tail plumage until it is seven years old.

ternoon to Pleasant Island in Icy Strait, just outside the park's southern boundary, to visit a 1,000-year-old hemlock forest, the climax to the succession story.

Heading up Glacier Bay to Wachusett Inlet, we retraced in part my winter journey. After a late spring, the mountains were still striped with snow, but the fresh perfume of cottonwoods just coming into leaf wafted from some of the slopes. Moreover—in pleasing contrast to my winter trip—there were all sorts of birds flying about or nesting on the beaches. We saw murres and murrelets, short-winged creatures that fish by diving headfirst into the water, using their wings when under water as oars. There were tufted puffins with large orange-and-yellow beaks, and a variety of ducks. But most exciting of all were the numbers of bald eagles. These magnificent white-pated, yellow-beaked birds— the national symbol of the United States—were everywhere. We saw them on the beaches, in trees, sitting on branches or in nests of sticks, gliding soundlessly through the air on wings that span seven feet—even riding on icebergs. The eagles are plentiful not only in the park, Greg Streveler told me, but all along the southeastern coast, the Alaska Peninsula and the Aleutian Islands. The eagle population of Alaska is estimated at 60,000, more than half of which choose to nest every year in Southeast Alaska.

The unexpected bonus of birds on our way to Wachusett Inlet inspired me to watch for animals as well. Though few large mammals dwell on the shores of Glacier Bay, some do come down to the water occasionally, bears especially. Two kinds of bears live in the park, the large brown and the smaller black. The park is also home to the glacier blue bear, a black bear that has a bluish cast to its coat. Unhappily we saw no bears, but we did catch sight of yellowish-white mountain goats on the nearly perpendicular slopes of 5,100-foot-high Mount Wright. Easily mistaken for boulders or small snow patches when motionless, they were hard at first to pick out even with binoculars. But once they began to scramble around on the ledges, it was not difficult to identify them.

Members of the same family as antelopes and sheep, these acrobats among mammals are so agile on the heights they inhabit that they are rarely the victims of predators. But they do not always live to old age. During hard winters many die from cold and starvation or from diseases brought on by their weakened condition. Despite the soft pads on their hooves, which give them traction, a few do slip from the icy precipices. The males, which sport large black swept-back horns, live by

themselves most of the year. The females also have black horns, smaller ones, and are more gregarious than the males; they tend to associate in bands, and we could see some on the heights, with their kids bouncing around them like flecks of wind-blown cotton.

Mount Wright marks the entrance to Muir Inlet, a three-pronged fork in Glacier Bay 30 miles from Bartlett Cove. We soon passed the site where the great Scottish-born American naturalist John Muir built a cabin in 1890. The glacier named for him extended this far at that time. Today its terminus lies more than 25 miles to the north, and the land around the cabin site is thick with alders. Icebergs, many bigger than the boat, floated by us, some glowing with a clear, blue inner light, others opaque and crusted with snow.

We veered to the left into Wachusett Inlet. On the rocky slopes at the entrance alders grow in patches. Their seeds had found all the little depressions and cracks and had sprouted. But once we had passed through the entrance to the inlet the alders vanished and a sullen landscape spread before us. The ground here had been free of ice for only a couple of decades and it was still raw, gray and lifeless. Black snow-striped mountains creased with gullies and ravines rose on the left, rock-strewn ridges on the right. The only real color in this monochromatic world was the occasional blue of an iceberg washed up on the beach like an outsized aquamarine.

We rounded a bend, and there ahead was Plateau Glacier. A formidable sight, it seemed about to surge forward and overwhelm anything—or anyone—in its path. As we drifted into the encircling arms of the ice, the air seemed to take on an expectant hush; it was easy to understand why the Indians had believed that in such places dwelled beings they called the Ice People. The curved front of the glacier was white, tan, gray and blue—the blue deepest in a spot where an enormous block of ice had recently broken off and created a broad pocket in the glacier. In this lapis lazuli cave a flock of gray-and-white arctic terns—tapered, streamlined, seemingly as light as air itself—flew back and forth, feeding on crustaceans and fish stirred up by the falling ice. To summer in Alaska these birds had flown all the way from Antarctica, and in the fall would return there.

We drifted as close to the glacier as we dared and then withdrew and went halfway back down the inlet. We set up camp 100 yards or so inshore on flat, pebbly ground from which Plateau Glacier had receded some 30 years before. The sun broke through the clouds, moderating the starkness of the gray realm that would be our home for a couple of days and prompting us to start our exploration of it without delay.

Actually, there was more life here than I had imagined. In wind-protected depressions, on clay outcrops and among rocks and gravel, plants were growing: buttons of green moss, strands of dark brown horsetail, occasional leafy stalks of dwarf fireweed just coming into scarlet bud, willow bushes, ground-clinging as well as upright, small cottonwoods and alders, and even a few stray spruces plumed with spring growth. All had come on the wind, as spores and seeds, and all had managed to sprout in this infertile soil, nourished perhaps by bird droppings or other bits of organic material. But what seemed so casual, so much a matter of chance, was not entirely so. For these are all species well-adapted for survival in a harsh, impoverished environment. Only they could successfully grow here. And as pioneers they have a role to play. They would prepare the land for new arrivals. Some would attract birds or provide homes for insects, and insects in turn would attract more birds—and eventually a host of mammals would follow, from voles and shrews to coyotes, mountain goats and bears. Birds and mammals would both enrich the soil with their droppings. Other plants, especially ground-clinging *Dryas drummondii* and bushy alder, would help build the soil; with the aid of single-celled fungi living in their roots, both these plants can take nitrogen from the air and reduce it to the nitrogenous compounds needed for growth.

In the natural order of things at Glacier Bay, *Dryas* precedes alder. It is a plant with small serrated leaves, silvery underneath, and a yellow flower that produces frizzy seeds the wind easily disseminates. *Dryas* has important work to do. It spreads rapidly and forms large interlocking mats that soon cover the glacier-scoured earth with a layer of organic matter. When *Dryas* dies, it contributes additional carbon and nitrogen to the soil. In its wake follows alder, a treelike shrub that grows and reproduces quickly. Its spear-point leaves, notched at the edges, are rich in nitrogen. When they drop, they collect around the bottom of the alder, caught by the branches that curve out from the base like arms of a candelabrum. There the leaves disintegrate, forming a fertile duff, or humus. As this duff gradually accumulates, other plants invade the alder's domain, including the species that finally suppresses it, the Sitka spruce.

Life on our beach was represented by other enterprising forms as well: tiny red mites, spiders, even an occasional bird. Near a felt-leaved willow—a bush draped with pollen-dusted catkins—we startled a male willow ptarmigan that had been feeding on the young leaves and buds. It chuckled gutturally as it strutted off, a handsome sight indeed. A chestnut-red cape of new spring feathers covered its head and neck, and was brilliantly set off by the older white plumage that covered the rest of the body; it still wore the fine, bristly feathers that grow on its feet in fall to help support its weight on fluffy snow. The bird seemed eager to have us follow it, perhaps because its mate and nest were close by; it kept turning around, attempting to decoy us. Among all the varieties of ptarmigan and the closely related grouse, only the male of this species is thought to assist with the rearing of the chicks, even taking over their care if the female dies.

To gain an overall view of Wachusett Inlet we climbed a ridge. The going was tough, with nothing but jagged rocks underfoot, and soon we were hot, our throats dry. Fortunately, we passed a stream that flowed down a narrow channel toward the inlet, and we stopped to drink from it. This was my first taste of "wild" water. It was cold and delicious; ever afterward in Alaska I was to quench my thirst by such means whenever I could. Few other experiences can beat the pleasure of kneeling at a swift-moving stream, seeing the rocks and sand through the clear surface and gulping the icy water as it slides off a smooth stone. Indeed, for me, the mark of true wilderness is no longer just a healthy animal population, but potable water—water so far from civilization that it retains its earth-given purity.

Refreshed, we stood at the top of the ridge. The clear light threw some of the glacial features below into sharp relief. Parallel rows of gravel marked the lines of Plateau Glacier's withdrawal; these were formed when the ice melted and the debris that had collected in crevasses sank to the ground. Horizontal bands in the face of the bluffs on the opposite side of the inlet had another story to tell. They were ancient streambeds. They had built up over the years, one atop another, with each successive change in the flow of the silt-laden water, then they had been cut through by the glacier. It was hard to imagine that the scene we surveyed had once been a forested valley and that it will be again within 150 years, when the revegetation process only now beginning here is complete.

Behind us stretched a sea of snow punctuated with crags. Two black-and-white snow buntings flew by, trailing notes of sweet song. How they could find enough to eat here puzzled me, but one item in their diet, Greg told me, is the segmented ice worm. This highly specialized

An oyster catcher, its red clothespin beak at the ready, casts a vigilant yellow eye at its world. Common on rocky beaches from Alaska to Baja California, this bird is misnamed so far as its northernmost haunts are concerned. Since oysters do not live in cold Alaskan waters, the bird feeds on crustaceans and mussels.

creature, an inch or so long, seems to live only in glacial ice and snow fields, where it feeds on wind-blown pollen, diatoms and the red algae that tint patches of the snow pink in summer. No one has ever found an ice worm with ripe gonads in Glacier Bay park; where it disappears during its reproductive phase remains only one of the many mysteries connected with it.

We returned to camp and after supper walked along the beach. A sea gull landed on a small iceberg and, to our amazement, its weight was enough to cause this chunk of ice to roll over. The gull flew off and then returned to the capsized berg, its perch now properly balanced; it stayed there for a good half hour, impervious to the cold of the ice. The temperature of the gull's feet, Greg explained, can go down almost to freezing with no apparent discomfort to the bird.

Many icebergs lay stranded on the beach, left there by the outgoing tide, and we strolled among them. With their smooth, glowing surfaces, they were like free-form sculptures, colored a marvelous blue by the low raking light of the evening. Some blazed white around the edges, others burned from within. But their beauty was of the most ephemeral kind as they drip-drip-dripped into oblivion.

On the beach, too, I met the oyster catcher—a bird that would become my favorite. It had a black body, yellow eyes, long pale-pink legs and a red clothespin of a beak. With stilted gait and bobbing head it patrolled the water's edge. When it spotted us, it let out a loud whistling "wheet!" and fluttered off. This alerted other oyster catchers and they joined in, all flying about madly. When they had become more used to us, they switched to another cry that sounded like Morse code squeaked out on a child's rubber toy. They kept this up until we walked away. At last sight, they were strolling down the beach, looking like old men with their hands clasped behind their backs.

The next morning the beached icebergs were gone, carried off by the outgoing tide. We started out for Plateau Glacier, using the pebbly beach as our highway. The nearer we came to our goal the more desolation there was. Plants were few and far between. In some spots, the vegetation consisted only of a black crust, made up of lichens, algae and fungi. But on one south-facing hillside spread a well-established mat of *Dryas*, about four feet in diameter, and unlike similar patches farther down the inlet, it was already in bloom. Astonishingly, the air several inches above the yellow flowers felt warmer than the air surrounding the patch. Apparently heat from the sun, absorbed by the ground and then radiated from it, had been trapped in the wind-free space around the leaves. In this warm microclimate the flowers had been able to come into bloom ahead of season.

While the signs of emerging life gradually dwindled as we approached the glacier, evidence of the old life—of the vegetation that had grown along the inlet before the glacier's advance—began to appear. A black clod of peat washed from a hillside was a section of the original forest floor; it contained decayed bits of moss, alder and horsetail. A similar clod a little farther on was serving as fertilizer for a particularly vigorous specimen of dwarf fireweed. A flat six-inch length of black wood proved to be an ancient root, compressed by the weight of

IN THE GLACIER'S WAKE, A SUCCESSION OF PLANT PIONEERS

DRYAS DRUMMONDII   MOUNTAIN ALDER   BLACK COTTONWOOD

the earth and ice that had covered it for 30 centuries. The root pointed the way to a deep stream-cut canyon; in its walls layers of gravel clearly marked the beds of other vanished streams. A waterfall splashed down steps of stone; on either side, still in place after some 5,000 years, were the stumps of trees. They had only recently been freed from the ice and looked remarkably well preserved after their long frozen sleep in the gravel. It was peculiar to be standing in the present, looking up at the distant past; it was even stranger to project ahead and imagine the forest that would grow where now the ancient stumps reared. But for the time being the only green thing to have invaded the area was a

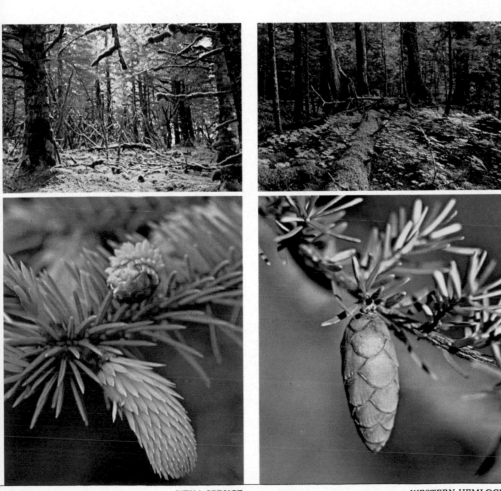

SITKA SPRUCE

WESTERN HEMLOCK

Land stripped of vegetation by a glacier is resettled by plants in a fixed natural order—the sturdy pioneers creating and conditioning the soil for their more complex followers. Five stages of this succession at Glacier Bay park are shown here in paired pictures—one a closeup of a representative plant species and the other of its setting. The first of these species to appear in large numbers is Dryas (far left), a rugged plant that can take root in sandy or rocky barrens and that soon spreads out in a low, dense mat (top). Meanwhile, bushy alders begin to crowd out Dryas, a process that takes about 35 years. Then cottonwoods move in on the alders and begin to overshadow them and cut off their sunlight. In turn the cottonwoods are overgrown by the taller spruce, whose rise to dominance begins in about the seventh post-glacial decade. The last newcomer to invade the maturing forest is the shade-tolerant hemlock, which can thrive in the shadow of the spruce and eventually replaces it.

long strand of algae. It clung to a rock and, like a tail, wagged back and forth in the waterfall.

Close to the glacier the landscape was in turmoil. Mounds of stone lay over ice that had yet to melt. Seemingly solid surfaces gave way underfoot, and our boots sank into the muck. To have ventured farther would have been reckless. Instead, we climbed a snow-patched hill and looked down on the glacier; backed up into the valley like a cornered beast, it had nowhere to go, and soon would shrink away.

The next morning we left Wachusett Inlet to travel five miles south to Hunter Cove on Muir Inlet. Hunter Cove emerged from the ice between 1910 and 1920, a decade before the area around Wachusett Inlet began to do so. It had long since passed through the *Dryas* stage and was now covered by a shoulder-high stand of alders mixed with willows. So thick were the bushes that walking was difficult. When I voiced my frustration I was told by Greg that I should try climbing one of the avalanche chutes on the mountains around Glacier Bay. There, because of the heavy snows that bury the branches in winter, the alders are permanently bent downslope, like so many prongs, presenting an almost insuperable barrier to the climber. At least we could see over these five-foot-tall alders at the cove, and we had easy footing. On the rare spots of open ground where the sun broke through, moss grew. Underlaid by sand, it spread a thick carpet.

Out on the beach again, we remarked on the sharp contrast with the naked shores of Wachusett Inlet. The ground around the waters of Hunter Cove was green with clumps of sandwort, its tiny starry flowers just beginning to open; scurvy grass, which the Russians, before Alaska became American territory, gathered to use aboard their ships as an ascorbic; salt grass, rye grass and other ankle-high colonizers of the shoreline. Absorbed in studying these many plants, we did not at first pay much heed to a bird that cried out at our approach. We had made the mistake of wandering too close to her nest, hidden somewhere on the ground. The bird, a semipalmated plover with a narrow band of black feathers around her white neck, tried to lure us away by pretending to have a broken wing, which she dragged pathetically over the pebbles. We stood stock still lest we step by accident on her eggs. When she saw us stop she became confused and, forgetting her ruse, flew up—only to land a few feet away and again try to distract us with the same trick. Afraid the eggs might cool if we stayed longer, we left, picking our way carefully back to the boat.

After lunch, we walked south along the beach. Soon we realized that we were being followed—by a seal swimming just offshore. Every once in a while it would bob up, take a quick look at us and dive. Occasionally it seemed to strain for a better view, rising in the water and exposing its spotted chest. We tried to get it to come closer by slapping the water with our boot soles. We thought perhaps this would whet its curiosity and induce it to swim toward us. But it would have none of our coaxing and kept its distance. At times it would disappear long enough for us to think it had deserted us, then would reappear.

Within walking distance of Hunter Cove we came upon an area that had been freed from glacial ice a decade earlier than the cove, between 1900 and 1910. Even the most cursory glance revealed what was different about it. Thrusting above the alders and willows were graceful cottonwood trees, one already tall enough to support the large nest of a pair of bald eagles.

In the Glacier Bay scheme of things, all was going according to plan. Alders and willows had succeeded *Dryas* and now cottonwoods were succeeding them. From this point on we saw increasing numbers of Sitka spruces. Spruce grows more slowly than cottonwood and alder, but it can get a foothold beneath them because it can tolerate their shade. It multiplies not only by seeds, but by sending out roots from drooping branches that touch the soil, and these form new trees that soon rise above the alder. This dooms the alder, which cannot thrive in shade. The cottonwood lives on awhile longer, being taller than the alder and thus in a better position to vie for the sun; but in the end it too succumbs. Then, as I was to learn later, the spruce meets competition—the Western hemlock.

While Greg paused to watch for signs of activity at the eagles' nest, I hiked up a small valley filled with rounded stones. Near a rushing creek I sat down to study the wilderness around me. To my right, a spring flood had sheared off the side of a hill. On top, alders clung to the crumbling edge, their exposed roots dangling in disarray. A few of the bushes had already plunged down the slope and lay sprawled and wilting below, partially buried by rock and mud. To the left, young cottonwoods advanced in a line along the upper bank of the creek, feathery and graceful. The new leaves glistened, and the buds were shiny with the resin that gives these trees their scent. In the cool, effervescent air the odor was refreshing and soothing. At my feet moss filled spaces between cobbles. Fingers of it reached around single stones. Soon it would cover them, attaching them to the earth. Here, as else- *(continued on page 64)*

A wary male mountain goat rounds the corner of a rocky escarpment in Glacier Bay park. When they are seen from a distance, male and female goats look alike; both have chin whiskers and shiny black horns.

Alaska's Champion Crag Climbers

The mountain goats that flourish in the soaring altitudes of southern Alaska, including the craggy peaks around Glacier Bay, are very contradictory creatures. They are large—a mature billy may weigh as much as 250 pounds—and their lumpy bodies, covered with a dense coat of white fur, appear clumsy. Yet they are the most nimble and sure-footed of all North American mammals—able to leap a 12-foot chasm and run 20 miles per hour on a knife-edged ridge. They have no trouble swimming a roaring mountain stream. At mating time the males make a great show of fighting over a disputed nanny—but almost never do they engage in serious combat.

The product of the mating also offers some surprises. At birth a kid weighs some six pounds, about as much as a house cat. But in a matter of days a newborn goat learns to follow its parents along the dizziest crags, and grows so fast that at three months it weighs 40 pounds.

A towering rock face on the shore of Glacier Bay (right) holds no terror for the pair of goats at top. The secret of their sure-footedness is a soft pad that functions like a suction cup under their concave, knife-edged hooves.

While her kid dozes against her flank, a female mountain goat lies placidly at the very edge of a precipice. With the onset of warm spring

weather, nanny goats produce one or perhaps two new offspring and also shed doormat-sized patches of their yellow-white winter coats.

where at Glacier Bay, I was profoundly impressed by the way life triumphs over the void, and by the relentlessness with which it moves ahead of death.

Returning to the boat, we sailed farther down Muir Inlet. Around 10 p.m., with the summer sun only beginning to set, we made camp on a sandbar diagonally across from Mount Wright and its goats. The site had been carefully chosen. The tide would rise around the sandbar, forming a moat that would keep bears from approaching while we slept. We were not being overcautious: saucer-sized paw prints in the wet sand near a stream where we had dipped a supply of drinking water indicated that a brown bear had passed by only hours before.

But the night passed without distraction by a bear or anything else, and we were well rested for one of the next day's objectives—a visit to a dominion of young spruces. Packing our gear in the boat, we boarded and resumed our journey down the bay. On the way we decided to make a side trip to a tiny island that is home to nesting gulls and oyster catchers. The intertidal rocks, fronded with seaweed, were encrusted with mussels, which these birds love to eat. The pebbly beach—in fact, the entire island—was littered with blue mussel shells picked clean by the birds. The gulls formed a worried, shrieking throng offshore when we arrived, but the oyster catchers did little more than fly from rock to rock, nodding and bobbing and communicating in their own Morse code. The gulls' nests—tidy beds of straw with four eggs neatly disposed in each of them—were easy to spot, but those of the oyster catchers took some effort to find. When we happened on one at last, its appearance seemed in keeping with the comical, live-and-let-live character of the bird. The nest was a careless dimple in the pebbles with some leaves of sandwort and some chips laid at the bottom, and in it rested a solitary egg. In the absence of the mother the sun-heated stones served as an incubator.

Just a few minutes' ride across from this island was another of our destinations of the day: a much larger island called Sebree. In its lushness, Sebree showed little sign that it had been under ice only a century before. Here all the successive stages of revegetation we had seen thus far had already taken place. The alders had grown ropy with age and, incapable of holding themselves upright any longer, were subsiding into a mossy tangle. In their collapse they had let in the sun, and the young spruces growing under them had responded by putting out new shoots. Other more mature spruces already reared above the few cottonwoods.

But tall as these spruces were, they lacked the moss buttresses characteristic of the still older spruces at Bartlett Cove. Nor did they have the reddish piles of scales that eventually build up around the bases of Sitka spruce as the red squirrel, chief denizen of the spruce forests, sits on the branches and endlessly shucks the cones for seeds.

From Sebree we went 10 miles southeast to one of the Leland Islands, two thirds of our way back to Bartlett Cove. The alders were well beyond senescense here; most, in fact, had died. The spruces had triumphed over them, spreading a dark canopy; beneath this, all that remained of many of the alders were long mossy branches, like so many ribs protruding from a decaying carcass. Except for these branches—and a few mosquitoes—we had easy going across the forest floor in contrast to the alder thicket area we had struggled through the day before at Hunter Cove. And when we emerged into the sunlight, there were flowers all along the edge of the forest: maroon-black Kamchatka lilies, fireweed, lady's-slippers, white goatsbeard, lavender vetch, strawberries, Pacific silverweed and many more.

Our next stop of the day was at Beartrack Cove, 15 miles southeast of Sebree. The cove was flanked on one side by tall spruces and on the other by a steep rock-faced mountain with trees leaning over the water. At the end of the narrow channel of the cove stood an enormous spruce, and high in its branches was an eagle's nest. The nest had been built above an older one out of which, incongruously, a red elderberry bush sprouted in full bloom. The bush had probably grown from a seed dropped by the birds and had found enough decaying matter in the old nest to survive. The birds warily observed us from their flower-adorned eyrie and then departed. Bald eagles almost always nest close to the water where they fish, and this pair had chosen to live not only right on the channel but also close to a narrow salmon stream that curves inland from the channel between deep-cut banks.

In summer, when the pink and chum salmon begin their runs to spawn, this stream teems with activity. Not only eagles but bears as well come to fish, trapping the swimming salmon with their paws. We walked beside the stream, its steep banks green with algae. The air was cool and utterly clear. On the opposite bank from us a broad meadow spread toward distant snow-capped mountains. We found a narrow spot upstream and jumped across. There we strolled among flowering strawberry plants, yellow dandelions and fuchsia shooting stars, surely one of North America's most exquisite wild flowers. Wide-skirted young spruces reared here and there in attractive groups as though they had been set out by a gardener. But there was ample evidence of the grove's wildness in the salmon bones and bear scat that lay strewed on the ground every 10 feet or so.

Back at Bartlett Cove, I could view the 150-year-old spruce-hemlock forest there with renewed appreciation. It was not, I now knew, the product of happenstance, but of a process that had been going on for two centuries, ever since the glacial ice began to recede. *Dryas,* then alder, had come and gone. At least 75 to 100 years had passed before the land began to be covered by spruces. Now those once small trees were 120 feet tall, their branches mittened with moss, their trunks bearded with lichens. But nothing is ever static at Glacier Bay, and spruces are not indestructible. When very young, they can survive under the temporary canopy of alders; but they cannot exist for long in the more permanent and darker shade of their own parent trees. Seedlings rarely live beyond a summer once they exhaust the food reserves of the seeds, and the rare saplings that reach maturity usually owe their survival to the sun that comes pouring in when one of the old trees topples over. Moreover, it is one of the ironies of the spruces' existence that their own falling needles help turn the soil acid. This provides a condition favorable to the growth of western hemlocks, which begin to increase in number. Their seedlings have the ability to survive in the shade that is hostile to spruce seedlings. As saplings, hemlocks play a waiting game, dwarfs among giants, until a spruce falls. Then in their own patch of sunlight they take over.

In the woods at Bartlett Cove, spruces still outnumber hemlocks. But outside Glacier Bay—beyond the area once covered by the ice—hemlocks dominate. To see this mature forest we journeyed from Bartlett Cove to Pleasant Island in Icy Strait. To get to the towering hemlocks we had to push through a wall of vegetation. Chief among the plants blocking the way was devil's-club, a shrub with broad maplelike leaves and long stalks that have barbs on them. It is well named: when clumsily shoved back, devil's-club rebounds and strikes painfully.

Once we had penetrated this perimeter, we confronted a tangle of smaller shrubs growing on the forest floor. But the real impediment to progress was the quantity of dead wood lying about. Over the centuries, trees had fallen on trees, and their rotting remains, piled up like jackstraws, were covered thickly with mosses that concealed pitfalls. For safety's sake we searched out the narrow trails of Sitka blacktailed deer and followed them.

Beyond the trees lay a muskeg similar to the one we had seen at Murphy Cove. How such bogs form in a stand of trees is only imperfectly understood, but they—and not the hemlocks—may well be the finale to the entire succession process. What happens, apparently, is that highly absorbent mosses spread over poorly drained soil, soaking up moisture and causing the forest floor to grow soggy. The water that accumulates eventually shuts off the oxygen to the tree roots, and the trees die. With their decay, the canopy opens and a muskeg is born.

On our way back to the boat, we were startled by the racket of cawing crows. They were chasing another bird through the branches of the cathedral-high ceiling of the forest. Suddenly we saw the object of their wrath, a bald eagle—and in its panic it let out a strange and wonderful cry, less a scream than a piercing creak. If ever one sound could sum up wilderness, it was this. As I stood and listened, some of the scenes I had witnessed in recent days flashed through my head. Again I saw almost-barren Wachusett Inlet, the alder-fringed shores of Glacier Bay, the cottonwoods, the young spruces of Beartrack Cove, the maturing forest at Bartlett Cove. I marveled that in today's world there is still a place where one can watch a wilderness being created. But what of the future? More than eight million acres of southeastern Alaska have been designated as federally protected wilderness areas. Here the forests live and die by nature's immutable rules. But elsewhere mining and timber interests have gained strong footholds. Power saws already bite into the ancient trees of the forests surrounding Glacier Bay. Here on Pleasant Island, the Forest Service has promised that no trees will be cut. And yet, as I strained to hear the eagle once more, the silence that rang in my ears was peculiarly saddening.

NATURE WALK /In a New Spruce Forest

At Glacier Bay National Park and Preserve, it is possible to observe at close range the fascinating process by which land once covered by glacial ice gradually, inexorably becomes forested. Each step of the complex process can be traced in the receding paths of surviving glaciers that are miniatures of those that once reshaped much of North America during the Ice Age.

The plants involved in the process are relatively few. Each in succession makes its contribution to the building of the forest. One prepares the soil for the other, and in so doing often creates conditions that are inimicable to its own development—and may even lead to its death. Among the first to appear on the bare earth are the mosses. Various species of these are the low-growing witnesses to the whole succession process. Other plants appear and disappear in an ordained sequence. Mat-forming *Dryas* is the first such plant to join the mosses, yielding to alder, willow and eventually cottonwood; these, in turn, give way to spruce; and spruce then yields its place to hemlock.

The last phase of the process has barely begun at Glacier Bay, but signs of it could be detected during a summer stroll I took through a part of the forest at Bartlett Cove, near the park's southern boundary.

Here in the 1790s stood the terminus of a 100-mile-long glacier. So ponderous was the load of ice that it depressed the land by several feet, and now the forested area around Bartlett Cove, park headquarters, is rebounding at the rate of an inch and a half a year, creating a rising shoreline in which spruces can get rootholds. But the young spruces of the beaches are overwhelmed by the much taller and older spruces within the forest and by a few slender Western hemlocks, the vanguard of the future. The forest spruces are mostly of similar age, having begun life together some 150 years ago and having triumphed over the alders that then covered the area. The spruces are also similar in size—about 120 feet high. They create such deep shade that visitors entering the forest from the sunlight of Bartlett Cove must pause to let their eyes adjust to the dimness. I had to do that when, one bright June day, I went there with Bruce Paige, a naturalist on the park's staff.

Just a few steps into the forest were sufficient to remind me of its origins, which are scarcely as old as

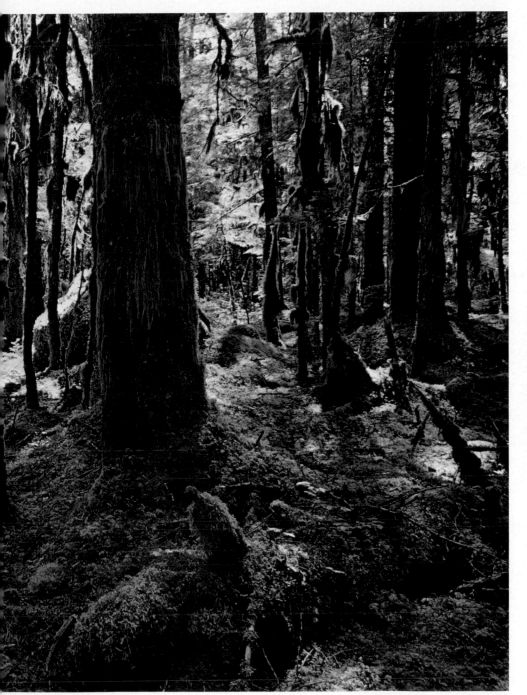

SITKA SPRUCE TREES

the United States Constitution. Underneath our feet the ground was distinctly bumpy. The uneven contours had been created out of the retreating glacier—shaped by the debris of rocks and sand it left in its wake. Here and there lay shallow, soggy depressions, marking spots where pockets of old glacial ice had lingered before finally melting away. An even more striking reminder of the huge ice sheet that weighed upon this land less than two centuries ago were boulders carried down out of the mountains by the conveyor-belt action of the glacier and deposited on the ground. Some leaned, as though about to roll over.

MOSS CARPETING THE FOREST FLOOR

But what struck me most, as I first looked around, was the preponderance of shaggy moss—not only carpeting the forest floor but covering boulders and branches as well. In places it was three to four inches thick, a soft, plush muffler that swallowed up sound and footsteps. It hung down from trees, and wrapped itself about roots and trunks. The very air seemed green. It was also damp, thanks to the 75 inches of precipitation that falls on Bartlett Cove in an average year. Through most of the summer, a week seldom passes without some rainfall.

As we moved deeper into the woods, it was apparent that while the darkness cast by the heavy canopy of foliage overhead encouraged the shade-loving moss, it inhibited shrubby undergrowth. Except for a scattering of blueberry bushes (favorites of the black bear in summer), there were few flowering plants. One of the most common and least conspicuous of these was a minuscule two-leaved orchid called the twayblade. We found it growing profuse-

A TINY TWAYBLADE MAGNIFIED

ly where light poured through one of the rare openings in the canopy. Only three inches tall, it had purplish flowers—so small that they were almost invisible from just a few paces away. Even up close we had to use a pocket lens to examine its delicate petals.

Such flowers produce seeds when fertilized by small insects. The seeds are so tiny that the plant must—and does—produce them in large enough numbers to ensure their growth in the moss, for the seeds can easily get lost in it and fail to root adequately after germination.

The moss is a deterrent to other seed-producing plants as well. They must rely on underground stems, runners or bulbs to perpetuate themselves. Ironically, in the struggle for survival on the shady forest floor, the spruce that towers over all eventually has the worst of it. Its seeds become entangled in the moss and rarely grow beyond the seedling stage, except when they take root on a rotting log or a patch of earth turned up by a wind-toppled tree. Moreover, the spruce needles, which continually rain down from above, alter the character of the soil to the detriment of the tree's own seedlings. The needles are highly acidic, and some of this acid—harmful to spruce seedlings—is washed into the soil as the rain water soaked up by the spongy moss slowly trickles down to the peat layer. Young Western hemlocks, on the other hand, tolerate acid soil, and they can thrive in the shade of the older spruce trees. This is why one day the hem-

TWAYBLADE LEAVES IN A MAT OF MOSS

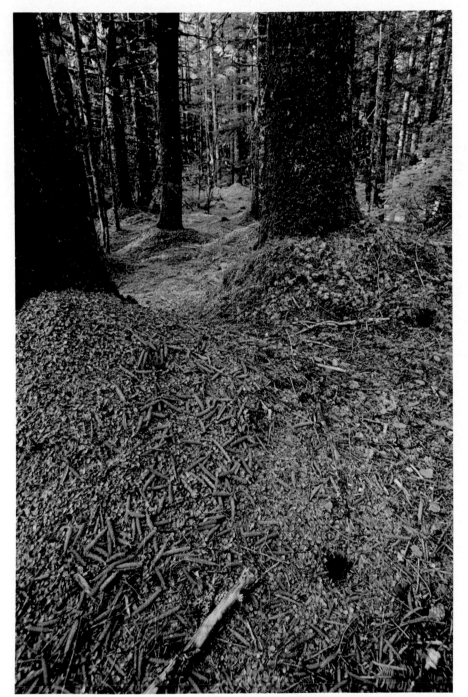

A MIDDEN—THE SQUIRRELS' LARDER

locks will replace the spruces, and the mature stage of forest succession will have been reached.

The Voice of a Squirrel

Meanwhile, however, the seeds of the spruces do not go to waste. They are an important item in the diet of a busy little forest creature, the red squirrel. The "chr-r-r" of this foot-long rodent is the one sound, other than an occasional note of bird song, that we heard in the stillness of the woods. By keeping a sharp watch on the trees, I was even rewarded with the sight of a red squirrel perched on a branch, tirelessly shucking spruce cones to get at the seeds. The bracts and cores of the cones fall to

A RED SQUIRREL

the ground and pile up around the base of the trees. Within these heaps of discarded material the squirrel hoards its winter food supply. In periods of severe cold it may also retire inside one of the heaps for shelter. Generations of red squirrels, shucking countless cones over the course of countless years, have built up three-foot-high middens, as such caches are called. Over these, in some places in the forest, moss has spread, giving the spruce trunks a firmly buttressed look.

Mosses often also grow in nooks and crannies of the shaggy bark of the spruce and hemlock, and we found them easy to examine simply by standing and scrutinizing the trees at eye level. One of the dominant species was fern, or feather, moss, so-called because of the laciness of its tiny leaves and stems. Another common variety we saw was the pendulous tree moss, festooning the spruces and draping itself eerily around dead branches in shapes that at times resembled animal carcasses. A third species, the weeping tree moss, dangled in filmy threads from the trees.

Interestingly, though these mosses are present in great quantity in the Bartlett Cove forest, there are not a great many varieties, a scarcity that is in keeping with the extraordinary economy characterizing plant succession throughout the park. As the succession advances, however, the number of varieties of moss will gradually increase.

Leaves That Drink

Lacking true roots, mosses can absorb moisture through their leaves, which are generally only one cell thick. During periods of plentiful rain, the leaves spread wide and drink in the water; they even absorb moisture from the air. But moisture escapes as easily as it enters, and during rare summer dry spells in the forest the leaves roll up, reducing the surface of the plants and thus preserving moisture by cutting down

PENDULOUS TREE MOSS—NOT A DEAD MUSKRAT

DOUGHLIKE TREE FUNGI

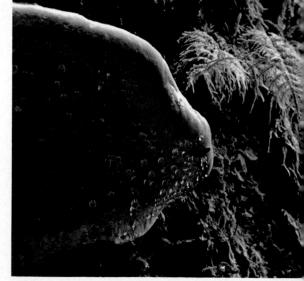

TREE FUNGUS OOZING MOISTURE

evaporation. At this point the mosses shrivel, turn yellowish and give the appearance of being dead. But when it rains again, the leaves reopen and turn bright green—and the Bartlett Cove forest once more becomes its usual lush self.

In addition to moss, the trees support a variety of lichens and fungi. *Polyporus,* a pale tree fungus, looks like a wad of bread dough fastened to the bark. It grows from rootlike filaments penetrating the wood, from which it draws sustenance. During its growth, it oozes moisture, which collects in tearlike droplets on its shaded underside.

Such parasitic fungi play an important role in the life cycle of the forest. In conjunction with other fungi, bacteria and insects, they help decompose the dead wood. Because the Bartlett Cove forest is, as forests go, still comparatively young, there is as yet little fallen wood lying about on the ground, and tree fungi have yet to appear in large numbers.

Far more prevalent are the lichens that grow on spruce and hemlock, ranging in color from gray green to gray, black and white. As Bruce and I walked among the trees I marveled at the many forms the lichens take. A few hang in beards or extend wiry branchlets into the air. Some cling to the trees' bark in crinkly, hollow arrangements that catch water. Other lichens look like crusts of peeling paint, or dried bird droppings. A few bear tiny cuplike fruiting bodies.

Lichens have neither true roots nor stems and leaves. They take moisture directly into their vegeta-

WIRY BEARD LICHEN

CRINKLY LICHEN

CRUST LICHEN

tive bodies, which are considerably more complex than they look. What appears to the naked eye to be a single plant turns out, under a microscope, to be two plants—a fungus and an alga. These have, so to speak, set up housekeeping together, and they derive mutual benefit thereby. The algal cells, embedded in threads of the fungus, contain chlorophyll; using the sun's energy, they manufacture nutrients through photosynthesis, and share these with the fungus. Through its gelatinous tissue the fungus, in turn, soaks up water—prodigious quantities during a rainfall—and gives some of it to the alga. It also protects the alga from desiccation; during dry spells, the same gelatinous tissue shrinks into a tough, moisture-conserving coat that covers the algal cells.

A Pond of Black Water

As Bruce and I moved from tree to tree, farther and farther into the forest, the dimness intensified. I had just about accustomed myself to its murky quality when we suddenly came upon a place where the light streamed in. This open area was Blackwater Pond, one of several ponds in the woods; each pond was created as rain and meltwater collected in a depression left behind by a chunk of late-melting glacial ice. Ever since the ice melted, Blackwater Pond has been slowly enlarging. Branches and needles fall into it from surrounding trees, clog the ground pores and retard drainage. As this material accumulates on the pond bottom, the water level rises —and increasing numbers of trees

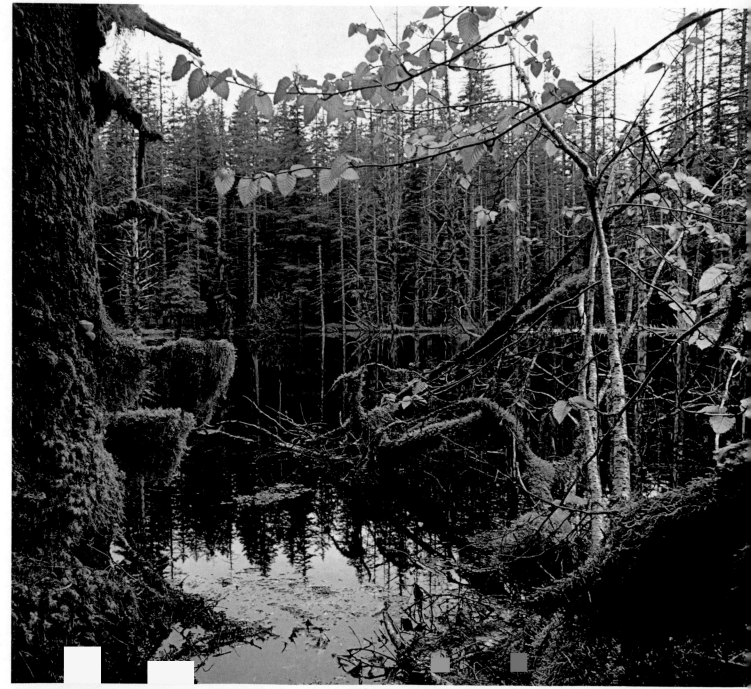

BLACKWATER POND—A FOREST OASIS

standing along the pond's edge die, cut off from the oxygen supply their roots require.

The rotting material has given the pond the characteristic blackish-brown color for which it is named. Along its shores grows a variety of plants. Indeed, a pond like this represents a kind of oasis in the forest. Because it is reached by the sun, it attracts both plants and animals. On the shores we found several stray alders growing; others of their kind had long since been driven from the shady part of the forest by the spruces. We also came upon a lone cottonwood, a survivor of an earlier stage in the plant succession.

A Prehistoric Plant

Rearing up from the banks were horsetails. These, which are among the world's earliest land plants, have no woody tissue; what stiffens them is the presence of silica in the cells of their stems. In the more tropical climate of prehistoric times, horse-tails grew as high as 40 feet; over the millennia they evolved down to their present height of a foot or so—proof of their adaptability to cooler conditions. At Glacier Bay National Park they represent a thread that runs through the entire succession story. They are found growing where the glaciers have only recently pulled back as well as in the alder and willow thickets, and they persist into the mature stage.

Besides such relict plants, the area around the pond contains several varieties of birds. Shy blue herons rest on the branches of dead trees. One rose and flapped off as we came close, its long legs outstretched stiffly behind it. Paddling in a shadowy part of the pond was one of the handsomest of all the wild ducks, a male Barrow's goldeneye, black and white, with a dark, iridescent head. Its less resplendent mate sat upon a log nearby. She had laid her eggs in a tree hole not far away, Bruce told me, but the ducklings were nowhere to be seen.

"Where do you suppose they are?" I asked.

"They may have been caught and eaten by a marten or a weasel," Bruce said.

Blackwater Pond is a good place to hear—if not see—some wonderful songbirds. We were lucky enough to catch the silvery tones of the hermit thrush, the species that so enchanted Walt Whitman that he acclaimed it "the unrivall'd one." The thrush's music came from somewhere in the trees, and echoed through the green caverns of the forest.

On this haunting melodious note we left Blackwater Pond and headed back through the trees toward Bartlett Cove itself. As we approached the shoreline, sunlight increased, slanting in through the wall of the forest. Dead alders, covered with moss, leaned toward us. Because of the light, these shrubs had been able

A FEMALE GOLDENEYE

THE VENERABLE HORSETAIL

SPINY DEVIL'S-CLUB

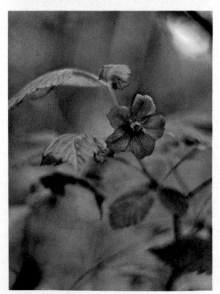

A SALMONBERRY IN BLOOM

to hang on longer than other alders deeper inside the forest, but had at last succumbed. They were all that remained of the original alder thicket that covered the area more than a century ago when the giant spruces were mere seedlings.

Also because of the greater light near shore, there was a bit more ground cover. Lady ferns arched their graceful fronds over the moss, and small blueberry bushes bearing tiny, bell-like blossoms stood here and there among the trees.

A Plant That Can Hurt

Near the edge of the woods the undergrowth noticeably thickened and became more varied. Devil's-club, a spiny shrub that grows in damp, partially shaded spots, crowded other plants with its big leaves and heavy stalks. We had to skirt it carefully to avoid brushing against its barbs. Just outside the forest grew another thorny plant, a salmonberry bush, covered with deep pink blossoms that would become succulent red and yellow fruit.

I had mingled feelings as we emerged from the woods—regret at leaving the lush darkness of the forest, yet relief at being out in the open again. From where we stood we could see the glittering waters of Glacier Bay, cupped in the massive fjord that had been carved by the ice; rising beyond the bay were snowy mountains, home of the glaciers. No one knows when—or if —the ice will come again. All that is certain is that some day there will be a hemlock forest standing where the spruce now rules.

LEANING DEAD ALDERS AND STANDING SPRUCE

3/ A Wilderness of Fire

Here was a volcanic outburst such as the geologist finds recorded in the rocks of past ages but has never before had opportunity to observe in the world of the present.

DR. ROBERT F. GRIGGS/ *THE VALLEY OF TEN THOUSAND SMOKES*

Some 700 miles due west of Glacier Bay, the land of ice, sprawls a land of fire—the Katmai National Park and Preserve. More than three times the size of Delaware, this 6,550-square-mile region at the base of the Alaska Peninsula includes one of the largest wilderness areas in the national park system. Few parks can match the breathtaking grandeur of Katmai's vistas. In addition to soaring mountains, deep glacier-gouged valleys, a dramatically wild seacoast, sparkling lakes and some of the largest bears in the world, it has seven active or recently active volcanoes. These belong to the Aleutian Range and are part of the so-called ring of fire girdling the Pacific from Chile to Indonesia. Along this horseshoe-shaped zone of instability in the earth's crust, earthquakes and eruptions occur more frequently than anywhere else on earth, often with disastrous results.

At Katmai, in June 1912, one of the greatest cataclysms of modern times took place. For two and a half days 33 million tons of rock exploded from the earth, radically altering the terrain for miles around and providing a showcase for the effects of vulcanism on a grand scale. When President Woodrow Wilson set aside the region in 1918 as a national monument, he did so to preserve for future study some of the weird and awesome features that this eruption had created—chiefly the steaming, ash- and pumice-filled Valley of Ten Thousand Smokes.

On a map, Katmai's boundaries, which have been expanded since

1918, form a benign image for so violent a place—they limn the shape of a fluffy chick with its head pointed eastward. The Valley of Ten Thousand Smokes lies just below its center. In what would be the chick's wing and tail there are several large lakes. Between the lakes and the seacoast to the south rise peaks of the Aleutian Range, some with glaciers descending through the valleys; one glacier is two and a half miles wide at its terminus. The coastline is indented by inlets, bays and lagoons, and offshore, in the waters of Shelikof Strait, there are rocky islands. The coastal beaches skirt jagged cliffs in which the surf has torn caves, and waterfalls tumble over the cliffs onto the sand and pebbles. In some places the landscape is richly green, especially where alders cover slopes with a tight jungle of growth.

For all its attractions, there are whole sections of Katmai that are still unexplored. From the air it is possible to see some of the wonders that await the intrepid backpacker—sapphire lakes, broad-shouldered mountains with deep, dark valleys, cataracts of white water crashing into black pools. For lovers of nature who feel that wilderness should exist in spite of, rather than for, mankind, Katmai is the ideal place. It makes few concessions to human comfort: some cabins and tent space in Brooks Camp and Grosvenor Camp, a few miles of rough trail and a single 23-mile-long dirt road that was bulldozed through the forest to give access to the Valley of Ten Thousand Smokes. It is possible on summer days to travel this road in a park van, one of the few motor vehicles in Katmai. Moose, wolves, foxes and bears use the road and spruce grouse sometimes sally onto it to powder themselves with dust and pick up pebbles for their gizzards.

The road cuts across many valleys. For a while, white spruce and cottonwood hug close; then the trees dwindle in number and the country opens up. Beyond a green knoll, one can see off in the distance a golden-pink strip—the lower end of the Valley of Ten Thousand Smokes. Dead trees begin to appear, barkless skeletons attesting to the 1912 eruption. The vegetation thins, and patches of white volcanic ash start to show up. Then, from the top of the knoll, all of the valley comes into view, a terra-cotta plain 12 miles long and two miles wide. It is flanked by mountains and blocked at its upper end by more mountains, including four volcanoes—Trident, Katmai, Martin and Mageik. Two rivers have gnawed deep into the valley, and the rims of the canyons they have formed are shriveled from the erosion of wind and rain. These weather effects are constants here, where the sudden, violent storms called williwaws rage at speeds of up to 100 miles an hour.

Before 1912 this was a green valley. Trees and bogs covered its lower reaches while tundra vegetation carpeted its upper end. Katmai Pass, lying between the mountains at the head of the valley, had been used as a trade route by the Russians during the first half of the 19th Century, and in 1899 by men seeking a shortcut to the gold-laden sands of Nome. From this pass had sprung the region's original reputation for violence. Winds sucked through it with tremendous force. During the unpredictable gales men were swept off their feet and dashed to death.

Outside of a few hardy sourdoughs, few people had ever heard of Katmai; to those who had, it was just another godforsaken corner of Walrussia or Icebergia, as Alaska was snidely dubbed. Then came June 1912. For several days tremors shook the area as the earth's crust responded to pressures building up under it. During one shock the face of Falling Mountain, at the upper end of the valley, gave way, and an avalanche of stone blocks rained onto the land below. On June 6 the earth opened up, and as it did, a brand-new volcano, later named Novarupta, was born. From its vent, not far from Falling Mountain, incandescent ash and pumice mixed with turbulent gas poured down through the valley in a froth that sloshed up slopes to a height of 900 feet or more and incinerated or carbonized everything in its path. So loud were the explosions that one was heard 900 miles to the southeast at Ketchikan. By the time the eruption had ceased three days later, more than 40 square miles of the valley lay buried under ash and pumice, more than 700 feet deep in places, and from fissures and cracks in the ash flow rose gases and steam—a phenomenon that was to last for years, until the volcanic material gradually cooled.

Had such a disaster struck in New York, the city and everyone in it would surely have been destroyed, and Philadelphia, some 90 miles away, would have been covered with a foot of ash. The Katmai area had few inhabitants. Those dwelling closest to the eruption, Aleuts, Indians and Russians in the villages of Katmai and Savonoski, had paid little heed to the first tremors. Living on the earthquake-prone Alaska Peninsula, they were used to an occasional shaking. But when the shocks increased in severity and frequency, the villagers began to flee. American Pete, chief of the Indians of Savonoski, and several followers hurried to rescue some hunting equipment they had cached at a spot in the lower end of the valley. They were thus nearby when the eruption started. Pete later reported to an American exploring the area: "The Katmai Mountain blew up with lots of fire, and fire came down trail from Kat-

The only road in the volcano-studded expanse of Katmai National Park and Preserve, described in this chapter, runs from park headquarters, Brooks Camp, to the Valley of Ten Thousand Smokes, relic of the great eruption of 1912. To reach other parts inside the park the wilderness buff must hike or fly in by light plane. The Katmai region, outlined in red, sits at the base of the Alaska Peninsula (blue area in inset map). The park boundaries are outlined by solid red lines. Dotted red lines indicate the park's designated wilderness areas.

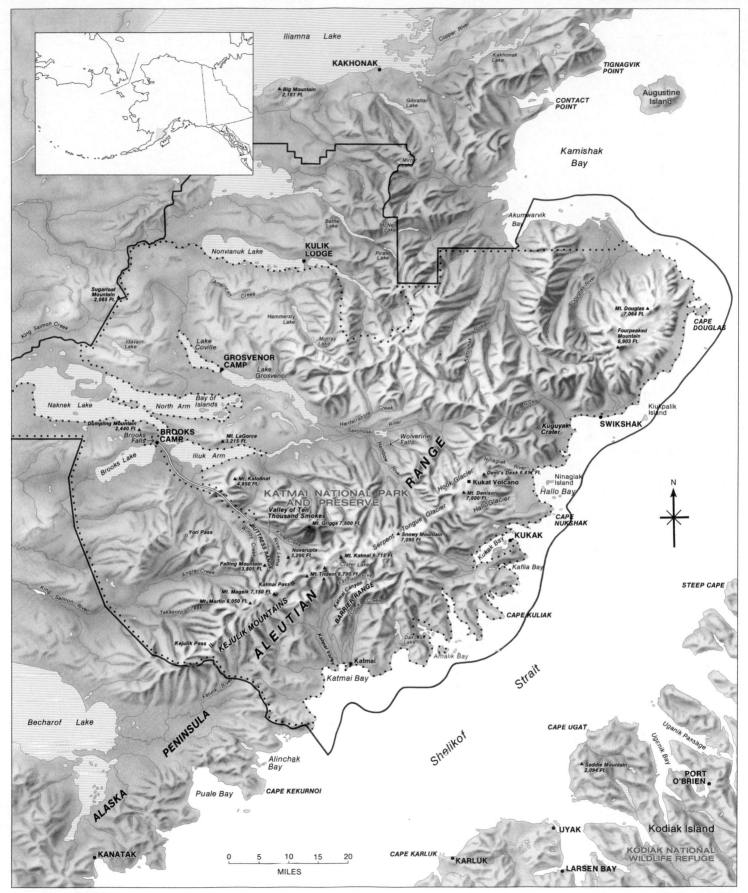

Iliamna   Lake

KAKHONAK

Copper River

Kakhonak Lake

TIGNAGVIK POINT

CONTACT POINT

Gibraltar Lake

▲ Big Mountain
2,161 Ft.

Augustine Island

Mirror Lake

Kamishak Bay

Battle Lake

McNeil Lake

Akumwarvik Bay

Nonvianuk Lake

KULIK LODGE

Pirate Lake

American   Creek

Douglas River

▲ Sugarloaf
Mountain
2,085 Ft.

Hammersly Lake

Mt. Douglas ▲
7,064 Ft.

CAPE DOUGLAS

King Salmon Creek

Idavain Lake

Lake Coville

Murray Lake

Fourpeaked
Mountain
6,903 Ft.

GROSVENOR CAMP

Lake Grosvenor

Kamishak   River

Naknek   Lake

North Arm

Bay of Islands

Hardscrabble   Creek

Big River

Kiukpalik Island

SWIKSHAK

▲ Dumpling Mountain
2,440 Ft.

Savonoski   River

Kuguyak Crater

BROOKS CAMP

Brooks
Falls →

Mt. LaGorce
▲ 3,215 Ft.

Wolverine Falls

Rainbow   River

Ninagiak   River

Ninagiak Island

RANGE

Brooks Lake

Iliuk   Arm

▲ Mt. Katolinat
4,850 Ft.

Hook Glacier

■ **Kukat Volcano**

Devil's Desk 6,414 Ft. ▲

Hallo Bay

**KATMAI NATIONAL PARK
AND PRESERVE**

*Valley of Ten
Thousand Smokes*

▲ Mt. Denison
7,606 Ft.

Hallo Glacier

Il Yori Pass

Knife Creek

Mt. Griggs 7,600 Ft. ▲

N

River Lethe

Tongue Glacier

BUTTRESS RANGE

Novarupta
3,200 Ft.

Serpent

▲ Snowy Mountain
7,090 Ft.

CAPE NUKSHAK

Windy Creek

▲ Mt. Katmai 6,715 Ft.

KUKAK

Falling Mountain
3,805 Ft. ▲

Crater Lake

Kukak Bay

Angle Creek

▲ Mt. Trident 6,790 Ft.

Katmai   River

Kaflia Bay

Katmai Pass

Katmai Canyon

STEEP CAPE

Mt. Mageik 7,150 Ft. ▲

BARRIER RANGE

Mt. Martin 6,050 Ft. ▲

Soluka   Creek

KEJULIK MOUNTAINS

Takayoto   Creek

ALEUTIAN

CAPE KULIAK

King   Salmon   River

Katmai   Valley

Dakavak Lake

Kejulik Pass

Amalik Bay

Katmai

Katmai Bay

Becharof   Lake

PENINSULA

Kejulik   River

Shelikof

Strait

CAPE UGAT

Uganik Passage

Alinchak Bay

Uganik Bay

▲ Saddle Mountain
2,094 Ft.

ALASKA

Puale Bay

CAPE KEKURNOI

Shelikof

PORT O'BRIEN

Kodiak Island

KANATAK

CAPE KARLUK

KARLUK

UYAK

**KODIAK NATIONAL
WILDLIFE REFUGE**

LARSEN BAY

0   5   10   15   20

MILES

mai with lots of smoke. We go fast Savonoski. Everybody get in skin boat. Helluva job. We came Naknek one day, dark, no could see. Hot ash fall. Never can go back to Savonoski to live again. Everything ash."

More distant witnesses to the eruption were aboard the small mail steamer Dora, as it was passing through Shelikof Strait between the Alaska Peninsula and Kodiak Island. The captain sighted a thick cloud rising from what he took to be Mount Katmai, some 55 miles away. The cloud increased in size, trailed the ship and finally overwhelmed it. Ash pelted the deck; darkness fell. Electric lights could barely be discerned a few feet away and crew members had to grope their way around. Windows were shut in the pilothouse, but thick dust so filled the room that the man at the wheel had great difficulty reading the compass. The captain set a course for the town of Kodiak but, unable to pick up the entrance to the harbor, he put to sea again. Fierce winds drove the ship forward, and throughout the afternoon and night lightning flashed and thunder roared—disturbances virtually unknown in this area. "In the saloon everything was white with a thick layer of dust," wrote the Dora's mail clerk, "while a thick haze filled the air. The temperature rose rapidly, and the air, what there was left of it, became heavy, sultry, and stifling. Below deck conditions were unbearable, while on deck it was worse still. Dust filled our nostrils, sifted down our backs, and smote the eyes like a dash of acid. Birds floundered, crying wildly . . . and fell helpless on the deck."

In the town of Kodiak itself on June 6, the ashfall—accompanied by thunder and flashes of lightning—began showering down at 5 o'clock in the afternoon. Soon night set in—in a season when there is no real night in Alaska. Static rendered the wireless useless, and later the station was struck by lightning, caught fire and burned down, cutting Kodiak off completely from the rest of the world. By morning the ashfall seemed to have stopped, but then it resumed at noon. Daylight disappeared, and the darkness was so complete and the ash so thick that lighted lanterns held at arm's length could not be made out. Sulphurous fumes hung in the air, along with choking clouds of dust.

On the second day the ashfall had still not abated. The captain of the U.S. revenue cutter Manning, lying at the dock in Kodiak, sent word to the town's priest that the terrified inhabitants could take refuge on board. Through the dark they came, feeling their way along fences, stumbling through ash drifts, their faces covered with damp cloths. About 500 managed to squeeze on board the Manning, which normally could hold 100, and others found shelter on the nearby barge St. James.

The *Manning's* captain decided that to stay in Kodiak could mean death. The cutter cast off, made its way through a narrow channel and anchored in the outer harbor, ready to make a dash for the open sea.

This precaution proved unnecessary. By the third day the ashfall stopped, and the refugees went ashore to assess the damage to their town. The ash lay 11 to 16 inches deep on level ground. It covered trees and plants. Some roofs had collapsed under its weight and some buildings at the foot of the hills behind Kodiak had been swamped by it. All this the returning inhabitants viewed with smarting eyes, for the moisture and sulphur dioxide in the air had combined to form sulphuric acid.

Here and on the mainland across Shelikof Strait, the immediate effects of the eruption were almost as terrifying. Hunger-crazed Kodiak bears took to attacking cattle. Fish died in streams, and cod, a staple of Kodiak tables, disappeared. The shellfish of Katmai Bay perished, and on the mainland most of the birds and animals were killed in the eruptions. Of those surviving, many were blinded by ash and soon died.

For at least a couple of years the results of the eruption were felt around the world. Dust blown 25 miles into the air circled the Northern Hemisphere and reflected and scattered the sun's light and heat. Skies glowed eerily over North America, Europe and Asia before dawn and after sunset, while sunsets and sunrises took on added brilliance. Solar radiation was reduced as much as 10 per cent, lowering temperatures an average of 1.8° F. and producing cooler summers and colder winters.

The first scientist to investigate the earthquake-devasted wilderness was George C. Martin, a geologist whose expedition was sponsored by the National Geographic Society. Arriving in Kodiak just four weeks after the great eruption, Martin gathered eyewitness accounts of the "hours of darkness" before crossing Shelikof Strait to the debris-choked mouth of the Katmai River. He spent two weeks studying the area around Mount Katmai, which was still rumbling and emitting thick clouds of vapor and ash.

Three years later a second expedition, headed by botanist Robert F. Griggs, reached the now-quiet site of the great eruptions. In July 1915 Griggs and a small party approached the mainland by boat through the Shelikof Strait. Uprooted trees and bushes and chunks of floating pumice still filled Katmai Bay, and ash made the lower reaches of the Katmai River unnavigable. "Over the sky was drawn a pall of fine volcanic dust which obscured everything above a thousand feet," Griggs recalled in his book, *The Valley of Ten Thousand Smokes*, "cutting off the volcanoes which we wished so much to see, and by its curious, diffused light heightening the unearthly aspect of the landscape, giving it somewhat of that ominous effect that raises one's forebodings at the approach of a storm."

When Griggs and his party went ashore, they found only desolation. Most of the trees were dead. A mystifying layer of sticky mud covered the broad floor of the Katmai Valley, reaching up the surrounding cliffs. Finding a campsite free of muck proved difficult; one possible spot was ruled out because it lay directly in the path of boulders that kept bounding off the mountains. The men finally pitched their tent on a relatively dry, flat bed of white pumice. The next day a dust storm blew up, limiting visibility to a few feet. The explorers' hair became so matted that they could not comb it, and sharp bits of pumice—a substance abrasive enough to grind and polish metal—irritated their eyes.

As they worked their way up the valley toward Mount Katmai, new hardships beset them. The only water they could find to drink was filled with pumice and ash; straining it through a cloth bag did not help very much. To climb the valley's lower slopes, which were covered with heaps of sand as high as 1,500 feet, they had to crawl on their hands and knees. "It was a treadmill," Griggs wrote, "in which one must either keep moving or be shifted to the bottom." As they sought a handhold, the fine pumice rasped their skin and ground their fingernails to the quick. At one point they came to a river ford filled with quicksand. They would have to cross it or turn back. They chose to cross it, going back and forth to carry over their equipment, sinking knee-deep as they went, despite, as Griggs put it, "the ever-present knowledge that we never touched bottom and the fear that next time it would 'get' one of us."

More trouble loomed after they negotiated the quicksand. They discovered that even seemingly solid ground often rang hollow. One member of the expedition struck his walking stick on the surface—and leaped back as the stick plunged through the ground into a deep hole. A closer look revealed that they were standing on a brittle, foot-thick roof made only of compacted ash; the cavern beneath had been formed by the melting of the snow on which the ash had fallen during the eruption. All around them they could see such cave-ins.

In spite of these dangers, Griggs and his party were fascinated by the Katmai Valley. At its head stood Mount Mageik, a three-peaked volcano capped by a towering cloud of steam. Next to Mageik reared another volcano from whose crater rose an even loftier column of steam, more than a mile high and a thousand feet wide. The maps did not show this volcano, and the explorers named it Mount Martin, for the leader of the 1912 expedition. Mount Katmai itself was not yet to be seen; other mountains obscured it.

As the party advanced up the Katmai Valley, the aura of death and violence intensified. There was no life to be seen anywhere. Ahead yawned a canyon that Griggs and his companions judged to be near at hand. But the closer they moved toward it, the farther away it seemed. They had underestimated both its distance and size. When at last they reached the rim, they calculated that the canyon was 4,000 feet deep— nearly as deep as the Grand Canyon of the Colorado. Close by was a puzzling red glacier, or something that looked like a glacier. Later they were to learn that it was a mudslide from Mount Katmai, at least 50 feet thick, and extending two and a half miles into a ravine.

From the camp Griggs and his men set up, they could now see the base of Mount Katmai, the volcano they yearned to climb. But they found their way blocked by the headwaters of the Katmai River. Tentatively they tried to cross the rushing current, using poles to steady themselves. It was all they could do to keep their balance. Fearing they would be carried away, or crushed by the boulders that were being knocked about by the current, they decided not to attempt to climb Katmai, that year at least. But they did not intend to be cheated out of a full view of the mountain. They waited three days for the clouds overhanging it to clear. They expected to see a peak. The mountain they saw was truncated— the entire top of the volcano was missing. The 1912 eruption, as Griggs later discovered, had demolished the top of Mount Katmai, reducing it from an estimated 7,500 feet to 6,715.

Griggs returned to the Katmai Valley with another expedition in 1916. This time they were able to cross the Katmai River. The climb on Mount Katmai's lower slopes was fairly easy, but the higher they went the more difficult it became. Dried mud gave way to slippery mud, and this, in turn, to soft snow. Again thick clouds obscured the summit, and the climbers arrived at the top before realizing it. At first they could see nothing. Then there came a little rift in the clouds that revealed "something blue, far, far, below." When at last the mist lifted, they found themselves perilously near the edge of an immense abyss created by the eruption—a caldera, geologists call it. "Down, down, down, we looked until the cliff shelved off and we could follow it no further." At the bottom lay a milky lake "of a weird vitriolic robin's-egg blue," with a horseshoe-shaped island in the middle of it. Steam puffed from crevices around the edges of the caldera and snow lay on the inclines. Later measurement of this cauldronlike cavity in the volcano showed it to be three miles long, almost two miles wide and 4,460 feet deep.

After a second ascent 11 days later and another tantalizing glimpse of the acid-blue lake, a buoyant Griggs decided to investigate some curious clouds he had spotted rising somewhere on the other side of Mount Katmai. In Katmai Pass he and a companion came upon a small fumarole, or vent, that was releasing a column of steam. A bit farther on they encountered more steaming cracks and fissures. Griggs was about to turn back when, from the top of a hill, they beheld a startling sight. "The whole valley as far as the eye could reach was full of hundreds, no thousands—literally, tens of thousands—of smokes curling up from its fissured floor. It was as though all the steam engines in the world, assembled together, had popped their safety valves at once and were letting off surplus steam in concert."

The next year, 1917, the indefatigable Griggs again came back with a third, larger expedition to explore his new discovery. The sight of the Valley of Ten Thousand Smokes, as he had by now named it, both overwhelmed and frightened his companions. Was it safe to explore—let alone camp in—such a spot? The ground often betrayed its fragility by shaking and hollowly echoing when the men thumped it with their walking sticks. The steam from the various smoking vents and cracks was burning hot, and the fumes were, in places, noxious.

Despite the threat of cave-ins and poisonous gases, the party established a camp and proceeded to explore the valley. The steam issuing from the fumaroles proved unexpectedly useful. The 1912 eruption had incinerated the surrounding forests, and there was no firewood anywhere nearby, so the men used the steam for cooking. It was more than warm enough to heat food: a thermometer thrust six inches into the ground registered 212° F.—the boiling point of water. Around the mouths of some of the fumaroles primitive blue-green algae and mosses were growing, the only vegetation to have gained a foothold in the valley in the five years since the eruption. These primitive plants benefited from both the warmth and the moisture of the fumaroles.

By 1919, when Griggs again returned to the valley, some of the smokes had begun to subside. Nevertheless, many fumaroles were still hot enough to melt zinc, and one, with a temperature of 1,200° F., softened an aluminum cup "so that it could be cut with a knife like pewter."

A pair of red fox pups spar in an open spot in a dwarf willow thicket in Katmai park. Fox pups play hard, wrestling and nipping each other until they flop exhausted, like the pup at right. The Alaskan red fox is larger and more richly colored than the variety found in the lower 48 states; adult males may weigh 20 pounds. Family life is close. Mates, once chosen, stay together and share the care of their three to six pups, patiently teaching them to hunt rodents and the foxes' winter prey, the varying hare.

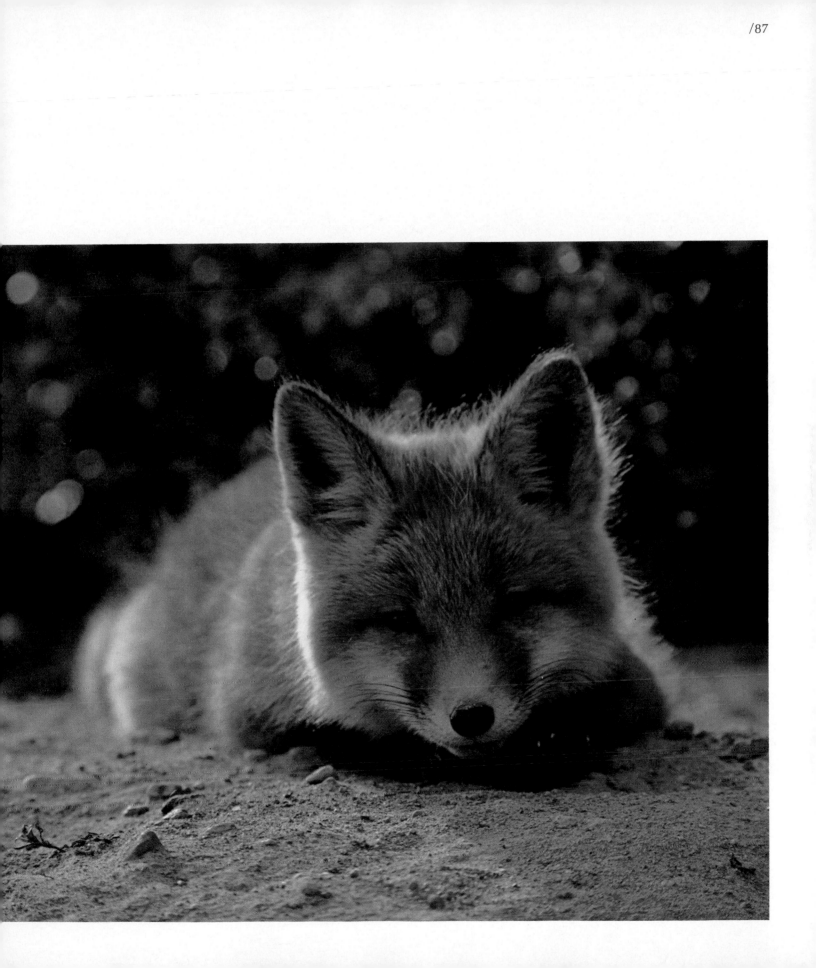

A stick shoved into this fumarole ignited. "Since the vapor was almost pure steam—that is to say, water—what we really did was to kindle a fire by plunging a stick into water," Griggs noted.

How, exactly, had the valley and its smokes come into existence? Griggs pondered the question long and hard before arriving at what he thought was an answer. He soon ruled out Mount Katmai as the source of the incandescent froth that had filled the valley on June 6, 1912, and had since hardened into the crust of the valley floor. Griggs's reasoning was sound: had this fiery, gaseous substance flowed down Katmai's slopes, the glaciers on the slopes would certainly have melted, but they were still intact when Griggs saw them. Griggs became convinced that the eruption had come from fissures and vents in the valley floor itself, chiefly from Novarupta, the new volcano six miles west of Mount Katmai. But if this were so, what had happened to the top of Katmai? Griggs considered the possibility that it had collapsed, but in the end he agreed with Clarence N. Fenner, the geologist who accompanied him on the 1919 expedition, that more probably it had been liquefied by the heat of the magma, the molten gas-charged material that underlay the area, and had then exploded in showers of ash. This theory seemed borne out by the fact that only very small pieces of original rock from Katmai's vanished summit could be found in the vicinity, suggesting that the rest of the rock had been transformed into ash or lava.

Since Griggs's day earth scientists have come up with another explanation for Katmai's missing top. It now appears that Griggs's first hunch—that the mountain caved in—may have been right. Dr. Garniss H. Curtis, a geologist at the University of California who has explored the area, thinks that Novarupta and Katmai had been connected by subterranean conduits, and that the new volcano acted as a parasite on the old, draining the magma from beneath Katmai and thus causing its unsupported peak to cave in. Thus, once activity died down at Novarupta, molten rock flowed back through the subterranean conduit to Katmai and pushed through the debris in the caldera to lay down a cone—the horseshoe-shaped island Griggs saw in the middle of the lake.

However it was created, the Valley of Ten Thousand Smokes is one of North America's most fantastic landscapes, appearing so extraterrestrial in its lifeless, dusty bleakness that it was chosen for the astronauts as a highly suitable place to train for their assault on the moon. Although almost all the smokes have gone out, there remains the pink pumice-strewn desert, surrounded by green and gray mountains, many of them snow-topped. To savor its otherworldly character you must camp out on it, as I did with a park ranger.

Our nylon tent stood on a stone ledge a few feet above the River Lethe, named for the underworld river of forgetfulness in classical mythology. Across the river were tan cliffs 100 feet high and coarse and pebbly in texture because of the ash, pumice and sand of which they are composed. Rain and melting snow have carved the upper part of the cliffs into a series of tapered buttresses that rose against the blue sky in a rhythm of sunlit protrusions and shadowed recesses. At their base, in the muddy water of the Lethe, small pieces of tan pumice bobbed about like corks. Where the cliffs curved back toward the upper valley, the river came full fury down a steep gradient, knifing through a cleft in the underlying stone only a few feet wide, twisting and turning and breaking into lace as it swirled against the smooth sides.

Exploring the valley from our camp, we confirmed what botanists had already reported—that the moss and algae Griggs had noticed growing around some fumaroles have since almost all died, and that the liverworts that appeared later have also vanished. But with the disappearance of these lower forms, some 40 species of plants have somehow managed to take root in the ash and pumice. We saw alders, willows and crowberry, among others. No one kind of plant was numerous, and almost all were leading a precarious existence on the edges of the valley, raked by winds, blasted by sand. Most survived in the shelter of fallen branches or of trees killed by the eruption, nourished by the slowly rotting wood in an otherwise sterile world.

Around the volcanoes at the upper end of the valley the land still seemed to be waiting for life to return. It lay barren, gray with ash. Rivulets had veined and creased the surface. There was a hint of brimstone in the air. The 200-foot-high lava plug of Novarupta rose from a crater of ash and pumice 800 feet in diameter, a gray blister dwarfed in the immensity of the landscape. Brick-red scabs of oxidized clay spread over extinct fumaroles. Mounts Mageik and Martin fumed. A pool of green bubbling meltwater filled Mageik's crater. Across the valley soared 7,600-foot Mount Griggs, the second tallest mountain in the park. Eight miles southwest of it we could see the rugged wall of Falling Mountain from which rocks continue to plummet. Behind other stony peaks Trident Volcano was visible. This peak has erupted several times in recent years; even during quiet periods it wears a vapor plume. Near Trident loomed Mount Katmai with its lake of vitriolic blue. Several glaciers sprawl on Katmai's western slopes. Covered with an insulating layer of ash, they are still unmelted even though they lost their chief source of supply and renewal when the top of Katmai collapsed and took the greater part of its snowfields with it.

Much has changed inside Katmai's caldera since Griggs first stared down into it in 1916. The water level has risen and submerged the horseshoe-shaped island, and on the inner slopes two glaciers have formed —among the few glaciers in the world whose beginnings can be dated exactly. The 760-foot-deep lake is fed in part by water that runs in wiry streams from snow melting on the rim and in part by snow toppling from rock ledges. The steaming has stopped, and the walls of the caldera can now be clearly seen. Its colors are intense. The brown and gray rocks are marked with perpendicular ribbons of brilliant snow. Part of a broad talus slope, the result of the slumping of one wall, is a sandy yellow, and strewn about it are red boulders. A wide slanting band of iron-red mud, curled at its edges, stands out against a ribbon of snow, and streaks of lavender and pale blue play through the cliffs.

But it is the lake that dazzles. The blue of its water is as vivid as a tropical lagoon. Where silt dissolves along the edge, a mustard-colored fan shape forms, and streaks of rust trace red whiplashes across the lake surface. Reflections of cloud patterns slide across the water, staining it momentarily dark blue, and in the middle a black bubble wells up and sends out ripples. Then slowly the mist closes in, floating over the rim and drifting down into the caldera. The lake disappears from sight and the air turns cold and damp.

The lake not only comes and goes from sight with the weather, but at least once it vanished completely. Clarence Fenner, the geologist who stood with Griggs at the rim of the abyss in 1919, came back in 1922 and was astonished to find the lake gone. In its place were mud flats, pools of shallow water and a geyser that hurled mud 200 feet into the air at one-second intervals. At other times the mud bubbled up in a huge dome and popped. Fenner looked hard, but could see no outlet through which the lake could have drained, and though water was still cascading from the heights into the caldera, it did not seem to be building up on the floor. Yet somehow the caldera refilled—and each year the lake deepens.

In a closer inspection of the area around our camp, the park ranger and I came upon the spinal column of a moose—the victim, we assumed, of wolves or bears. The animal had been picked clean, and bones lay scattered about under a bush. Wolves are not uncommon in the park but they seldom reveal themselves to human beings. Not long ago, however, two wolves boldly stalked a young moose under the eyes of a group of visitors to the valley. The wolves managed to bring the moose down, fed for a while on the carcass and then abandoned it, perhaps aware they were being watched or perhaps simply leaving it to return for another meal, as wolves often do. But before they could return two brown bears discovered the carcass and finished it off.

Brown bears are far more numerous than wolves in the park, and a great deal more conspicuous. We had plenty of signs of their presence right around our camp—from pawprints and scat to well-worn trails skirting the cliffs. And as these signs made only too plain, the brown bears of Katmai are formidable creatures. Both the brown bear and the grizzly are members of the species *Ursus arctos,* but the brown bears are usually bigger. A big male can weigh 1,500 pounds, or almost three times as much as a lion, and rear nine feet high on hind feet that are 14 inches long. There is no larger carnivore in the world, except perhaps the polar bear. Victor Cahalane, former chief biologist of the National Park Service, tells a story that illustrates the bear's tremendous strength. Cahalane and the biologist George B. Schaller came upon the 1,000-pound carcass of a moose floating in a river. Thinking it would make good bait for bears they wanted to photograph, they tried to haul it from the water with ropes, but they could move it only as far as the shallows. The next night a bear found the carcass, easily pulled it out of the water and buried it in gravel—bears often cache their meat. The next evening Schaller went back, hoping that the bear would return. From his perch in a large spruce he watched as a medium-sized brown bear lumbered up, grabbed the moose's hindquarter with its teeth and, with a single quick jerk of its head, yanked the carcass from the gravel.

The Katmai bears, like bears everywhere, are creatures of habit. Invariably they tread the same trails year after year. Some of these are cut five and six inches deep, and around park headquarters at Brooks Camp, where moss lies thick, individual pawprints show up so distinctly and are so evenly spaced that a man can walk in them and experience something of the rolling gait of the animals themselves.

The bears have three gaits: an even, deliberate one that takes them over rough or boggy ground at a steady three-mile-an-hour clip; a quick shuffle; and a 20- to 25-mile-an-hour gallop. They are not only surprisingly fast, but also, for such huge beasts, amazingly agile. They can charge up precipitous slopes and climb down nearly vertical inclines. Fishing the streams in June, July and Au- (continued on page 96)

Brown bears gather to fish for salmon on McNeil River, north of Katmai park; gulls from the nearby sea will scavenge leftover bits.

The Salmon-fishing Bears of Alaska

The great brown bears of Alaska are, with polar bears, the biggest flesh-eating animals on earth, and feast sumptuously in summertime when salmon swim up Alaska's rivers to spawn. Bears lumber out of the surrounding shrubs and make for the swift, shallow rapids, where the salmon, exhaustedly fighting upstream against white water, are easy pickings. A bear simply wades into the stream, pinions a four-to-six-pound salmon with its sharp-clawed paws and devours it.

Brown bears are found in Alaska and the neighboring parts of western Canada—the Yukon Territory and British Columbia. They are found mainly in the part of the Alaska Peninsula that includes Katmai National Park and Preserve and on Kodiak Island offshore. Having slept through most of the long Alaskan winter, the brown bears and their newborn cubs emerge in April to search for food. Almost anything will do —young grass, shoots or even a beached whale carcass—until the salmon begin to run. Then the bears gorge themselves. As many as 80 bears have been observed at the McNeil River falls near Katmai park, one of their favorite fishing spots.

There a hungry bear has been known to catch and eat 40 pounds of fish in an hour. When the orgy has ended, the biggest males have filled out to 1,500 pounds and all of the brown bears have the fat they will need to go through another winter.

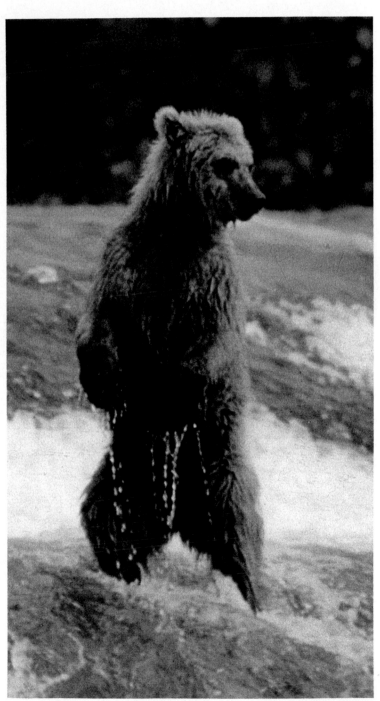

Losing a fish in a rapids, a big male droops empty, streaming paws.

Carrying a salmon, a female brown
bear heads for shore with three hungry
cubs in tow. Cubs are born in winter.
Helpless and furless 12-ounce mites
at birth, they fatten to eight pounds
on their mother's milk before she
leads them from the den in April or
May. Then she watches over them
attentively for at least two years,
training them to be self-sufficient.

A massive brown bear uses its long
pointed claws and teeth to tear into a
salmon's pink flesh. A bear may eat
as many as eight salmon for one meal,
catching them one after another.
Then, made sleepy by this fish orgy, the
bear will pad off into the woods to
nap until its appetite revives.

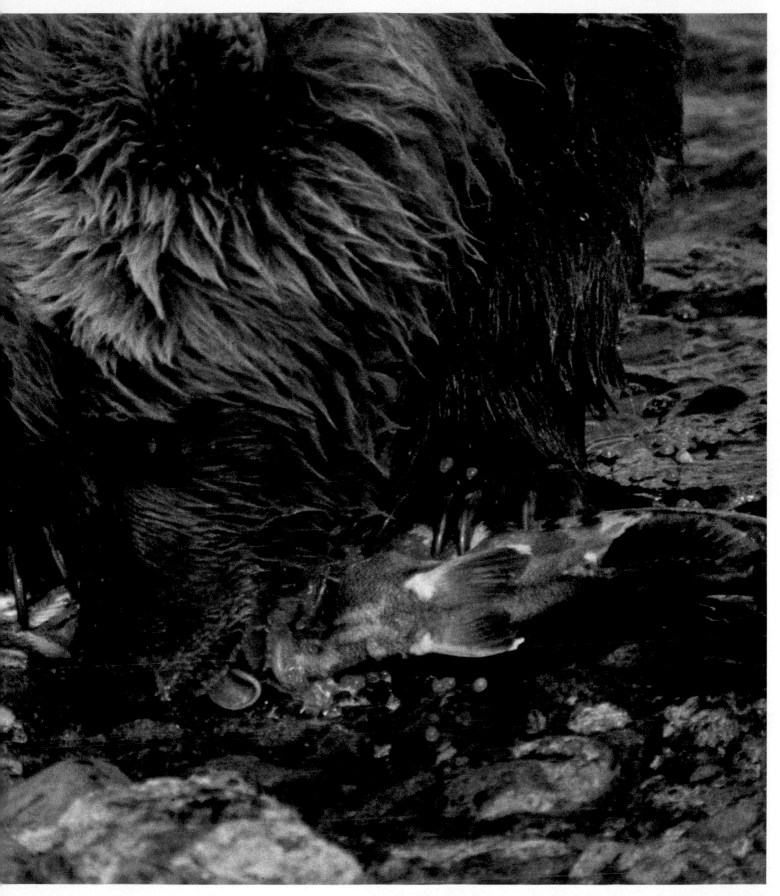

gust, they pounce on salmon struggling upstream to their spawning sites and catch them with almost simultaneous movements of their paws and mouths. They then bring the fish to shore clamped in their jaws, pinion them on the ground with a paw and rip off chunks of the pink flesh.

Bears also have a fierce sense of hierarchy; when fishing, the largest and oldest bears command the spots where the salmon are easiest to catch. The other bears wait their turn or fish other parts of the stream. If its prerogatives are challenged, an older bear can react violently. A few years ago at Brooks River, near Brooks Camp, a young bear made the mistake of venturing into an elder's domain. The larger bear lunged at the interloper, disemboweled it and then drowned it. All this happened in full view of three fishermen, one of whom filmed the event. At the end they watched dumfounded as the big bear dragged the soaking body of its victim 25 feet up the embankment and buried it.

For all their ferocity, the brown bears and the closely related Kodiak bears are not without a degree of charm. They are good swimmers, and apparently love to loll and wallow in the water on warm days. Cahalane spotted one from a helicopter floating on its back in a pool with all four legs spread out. Will Troyer and Richard Hensel, former managers of the Kodiak National Wildlife Refuge, report that the brown bears there, just like their caged brothers in hot and crowded zoos, often soak in pools during heat spells, with only their heads showing. Troyer and Hensel say that even mature bears are given at times to playful moods, although the young do most of the cuffing and wrestling. Troyer saw one large bear slide down a snowbank again and again, just like a child. On another occasion a guide watched as a female with cub rolled a snowball along a slope. When it fell into a ravine she became enraged.

In sleep these giants present a picture of utter relaxation. They often bed down where the air currents will keep them informed about any interlopers. They sleep in one of several casual positions—curled up like a dog with head resting on paws, or stretched out on their sides, or flat on their backs with their feet up in the air.

The bears in Katmai park manifest a fear of man, and will usually flee at the whiff or sound of a human being. Still, the rangers caution visitors about walking on the paths around Brooks Camp. Their advice is to step aside slowly should a bear approach from the opposite direction, and let it pass. Apparently the best defense against a bear is not to startle it but to let it gradually become aware of you. Still, there is no way of knowing when a bear might come charging at you. Frank Dufresne, an old Alaska hand, describes such a situation in his book, *No Room for Bears.* He says: "Nobody guarantees what will happen, but if you can stand your ground quietly, if you can hide the quaver in your voice while you talk to the bear in moderate tones, if you can put on a convincing show of calmness and firmness, the bear's temper *might* suddenly soften. Having given you the business of buttoned-down ears, popping teeth, foaming jaws, belly-deep whuffs and moans, a change *may* come over the shaggy ogre. The ears may snap forward alertly, the big head may cock sideways like a friendly dog's; the bear may, repeat *may*, stroll away feigning complete indifference."

Alaskans in general are careful to give bears advance warning of their presence, often by carrying a noisemaker of some kind, such as a whistle or a tin can filled with pebbles. In the valley I wore a small brass bell attached to my belt and felt more easy about following a bear trail through some low brush to an open area at the edge of the ash flow, where I could look down on the confluence of the River Lethe and Knife and Windy Creeks. Here the Valley of Ten Thousand Smokes has been worked by water and carved into a broad canyon, complete with mesas and small caves. No alders or willows graced the rocky banks, no moss clung to the red rocks. The only living thing was the water itself. Yet close by were pawprints. Why bears would visit such a barren spot was puzzling unless, like myself, they did so out of curiosity—and bears do have this curiosity. When I looked up, I jumped at the sight of two bears advancing across the valley in my direction. Fortunately, they were a half mile away, too far off to pose any danger. I was as safe as I had been once in a plane that flew over seven bears that were crossing a meadow near the Katmai coast. Startled by the roar of the plane, the seven of them ran with surprising speed and tore effortlessly up a steep incline into the brush. In this display of agility and power they struck me as the only living things that could possibly measure up to the magnificence of Katmai itself.

The Valley of Ten Thousand Smokes

Among the most convulsive corners of the earth is the volcano-studded Alaska Peninsula, and one of the most dramatic displays of the power of its restless mountains may be seen at its eastern end, in Katmai National Park and Preserve. Within this 6,550-square-mile area volcanic seethings are constantly present, as the picture opposite shows. Katmai also contains a massive reminder of the explosive force that the earth could—and once did—unleash: the Valley of Ten Thousand Smokes.

Katmai's colossal blowup took place in June 1912, altering the area's landscape, spreading ash and sulphurous gases over 42,000 square miles and eventually darkening and cooling the entire Northern Hemisphere with the nearly seven cubic miles of volcanic ash the eruption blew into the air.

Despite the magnitude of the cataclysm, no deaths are known to have occurred, thanks to the Katmai region's thinly scattered population. Because there were no more than a few eyewitnesses, the sequence of events was uncertain for many years. The first reports placed the epicenter at 7,500-foot-high Mount Katmai. "The top of Katmai blun off," said one survivor. Today, however, most geologists are convinced that it was not Mount Katmai but a new volcano located six miles to the west—appropriately named Novarupta—that suddenly burst, spewing pumice and fragments of rock; and that in the following breath Novarupta vomited a frothing mass of incandescent ash.

This scorching avalanche smothered a 12-mile-long valley under an ash blanket that reached depths of 700 feet. Glacial ice, streams and ponds buried under the hot blanket turned to steam that forced its way upward through thousands of fissures, or fumaroles, in the ash. At some time during the eruption, the top of Mount Katmai collapsed, probably because its supporting core of magma was siphoned off by Novarupta through a network of subterranean conduits.

The first scientists to explore the ash-smothered valley were awed by the sight of its myriad plumes of steam, which prompted botanist Robert Griggs to name it the Valley of Ten Thousand Smokes. Steam no longer shrouds the valley, but—as the following pages show—the effects of rampaging nature remain to astonish the few who venture into this wasteland.

Steaming vents inside Mount Martin's crater at Katmai park testify to the volcano's explosive potential. Clifflike walls of layered ash and pumice, thrown off by past eruptions, surround the cone-shaped chasm. Volcanic outbursts such as this are common to the Katmai area, which is one of the earth's most unstable regions.

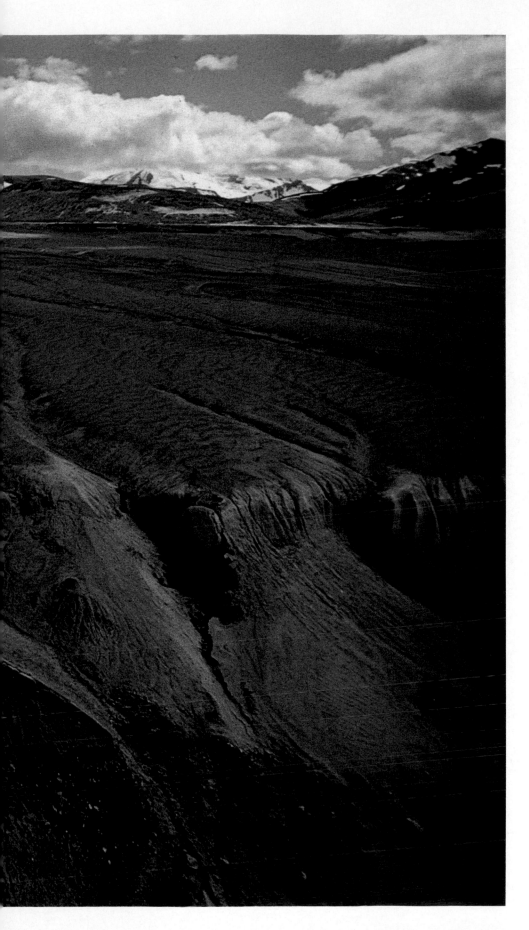

An air of eerie unreality pervades
the Valley of Ten Thousand Smokes,
pictured here at its lower end, with
the Buttress Range in the background.
Denuded of vegetation, its ash-dust
floor gashed by tortuous streams, this
bleak place no longer steams with
the vapor plumes that gave it its name.
The thick layers of ash, long since
cooled, have contracted and gradually
fractured. Erosion by rain and water
from melting glaciers further scarred
the surface with crevices. Into these
poured river water, including the flow
from the Knife River (far left), which
has cut through at least nine layers of
compressed ash to form a deep
canyon. The valley surface, once
perilously thin and fragile in places,
is now firm enough to hold a walker's
weight without danger of collapsing.

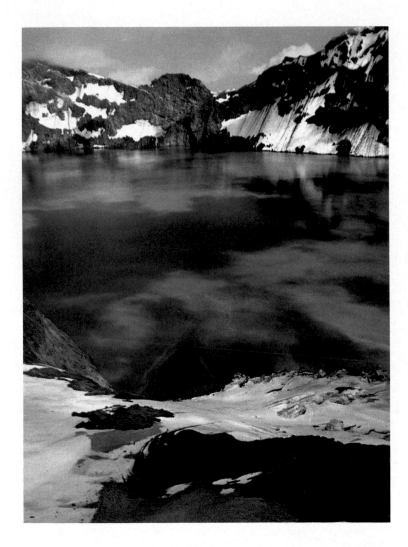

A lake 760 feet deep now fills the crater of Mount Katmai (left), where molten rock used to bubble. The once lofty peak caved in when the eruption of nearby Novarupta in 1912 siphoned off its underlying magma. The immense caldera that resulted—a hole six miles square and four fifths of a mile deep—gradually filled with water. On the region's few clear days the vivid ultramarine water mirrors snow-covered slopes and ever-changing cloud patterns. Rusty streaks on the lake surface are caused by particles of ash dust containing iron, remnants of volcanic ejecta that are washed down from the rim into the crater by rain and melting snow.

Six miles upvalley from Mount Katmai, Novarupta's crater (right) lies peacefully in a setting of white-capped crests. The 200-foot-high dome at its center consists of magma thrust up from the earth's depths during the volcano's last surge. Now serving as a mammoth plug, the dome seals the volcano's vent and permits only an occasional plume of steam to escape. Thick deposits of ash and pumice disgorged during the eruption cover the rim of the bowl. Only 800 feet in diameter, the crater seems incredibly small to have produced one of the most cataclysmic outbursts on record.

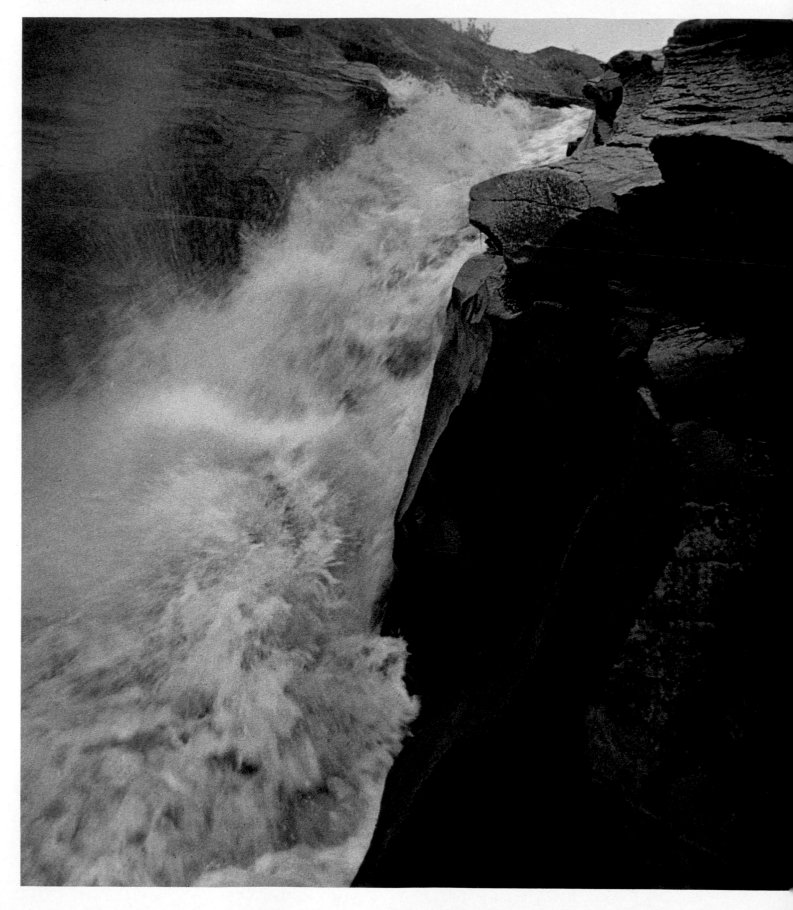

Torrential waters of the River Lethe (left) plunge through a channel near the lower end of the Valley of Ten Thousand Smokes. This violent flow is fed by water from thawing glaciers, melting snow and the valley's heavy precipitation. The muddy color of Lethe—named after one of the five mythological rivers of Hades—is produced by volcanic ash and bits of pumice mixed with sand and silt released from glaciers. The presence of these particles greatly increases the water's power to erode. Over a comparatively short span of years it has gnawed its way down to the lowest layer of the volcanic ash flow.

Resembling the flying buttresses of a Gothic cathedral, riblike cliffs 100 feet high (right) loom over the River Lethe. These formations, composed of yellowish-gray ash and pumice, are what geologists call "badlands topography"—a description inspired by their stark, barren look. Years of erosion produced these strange sculptures. As rain and spring meltwater flowed over the escarpment walls, the weaker parts of the rock surface were carved more deeply, sharpening the ridges between.

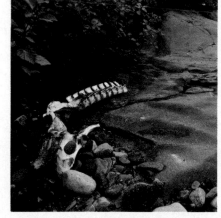

Signs that life has begun to take hold once more are evident here and there in the Valley of Ten Thousand Smokes. The remains of a moose (above), probably killed by hungry wolves or bears, rest near a patch of new greenery. In the panoramic view at right, similar patches denote various stages of revegetation. Greenish-gray mosses in the foreground form a network of rounded clumps across the surface. Beyond them are scruffy willow bushes and the taller hardy alder. These plants are not yet abundant enough to lend much color to the ash-dusted earth, but they already provide food for foraging moose—food that cannot be found on the sterile ash plain atop the cliffs in the background. At the foot of these bleak red-brown cliffs, which mark the abrupt end of the ash flow of 1912, is the River Lethe—not visible in this picture.

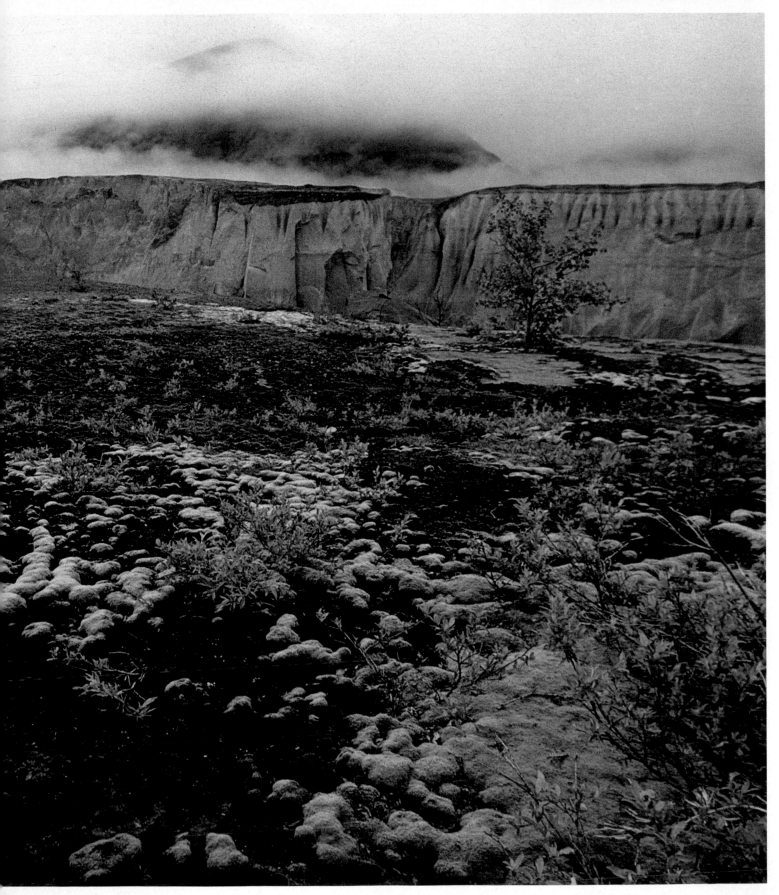

4/ A World in Delicate Balance

Wilderness without its animals is dead — dead scenery.
Animals without wilderness are a closed book.

LOIS CRISLER/ *ARCTIC WILD*

It is 10 p.m. in Denali National Park and Preserve on the longest day of the year—a June day that will here have no end. Sunset at 11:37 p.m. will be followed by two hours and 28 minutes of twilight, the twilight by dawn at 2:05 a.m. From where I stand in the valley near Stony Hill, "The Mountain," as Alaskans simply call Mount McKinley, is 36 miles away. It looms against a pale sky, the highest eminence in North America, a 20,320-foot mass of jagged granite swathed most of the summer in clouds. The peak, pyramidal in shape, rises from rank on rank of lesser pyramids in the Alaska Range, the 600-mile-long dividing line between the southern portion of the state and the interior. From this distance McKinley seems two-dimensional, its overall whiteness tinted a lambent blue, lavender and gold by the evening light. Yet, the tundra down here in the valley and the surrounding hills lie dark and wet from a recent rain. The wind blows hard.

Animals are about. A red fox, its fur soaked, an arctic ground squirrel dangling from its jaws, steps from a patch of dwarf birch. Its expression is intensely alert as it heads for its den where vixen and pups await the meat it brings. A golden eagle wheels high in the sky, and a long-tailed jaeger, a large bird of prey with a black head and gray body, dives down toward its quarry on the tundra like a kite gone out of control. A mother grizzly ambles across a slope, trailed by a cub that pauses from time to time to take a bite of fresh, juicy grass. The low rays of the sun strike the bears from behind and throw halos around their tan fur. On another slope two caribou break into a trot. One is a male, scruffy in a shedding winter coat, but with growing antlers covered in the new soft skin known as velvet, its texture as plushy as the catkins dangling from willow bushes close by.

Although summer began today, there is still snow on the ground, filling depressions in the tundra, and rivers and streams run agitatedly, with an icy mix of melt-off and muddy rain water. But the snow is mostly history now; the heat and light of the sun are at their life-giving best. Within the past few weeks here, under the sun's rays, animals have been born, plants have sprouted, insects have sprung to life. The golden plover has arrived from Hawaii to lay its eggs in hollows in the ground; for Alaskans its plaintive call, carried by the wind, is a cry of spring. The wheatear has flown in from Asia, the surfbird and the wandering tattler from the far south, joined by dozens of other migratory birds that make their nests here during summer.

Wakened only a month ago from its frozen nine-month winter torpor, the gray-green tundra is now a busy, lively place, dotted everywhere with yellow, pink, blue, white and lavender flowers; but in another month it will already have acquired the first bold daubs of autumn coloring. By late August, it will be russet, gold and red; by late September it will have turned brown, or perhaps even white, dusted with the earliest flurries of snow. Living things must therefore hurry to get the work of growing and reproducing done before winter returns. Only some will make it. Many, like the ground squirrel in the fox's mouth, will have been sacrificed along the way.

The struggle for survival that takes place during this short season is only one of the fascinations of Denali park. Comprising 8,900 square miles of mountainous and rolling terrain, the park lies in Alaska's interior between Fairbanks and Anchorage and some 175 miles south of the Arctic Circle. Because Mount McKinley and other peaks of the Alaska Range cut off most of the southerly moisture-bearing winds, a large part of the park has a relatively dry though severe winter climate and broad expanses of tundra.

In these open areas one can easily observe links in the chain of life. The first link is the sun; the second, the vegetation that draws upon the sun's energy and converts it through photosynthesis into energy of its own. The third link consists of those creatures that feed upon the plants. And the fourth consists of the animals that consume the plant eaters. Since the northern sun shines strongly only part of the year, this transfer of the sun's energy reflects a simple equation—the fewer days of sunshine there are, the fewer plants there can be; the fewer plants, the fewer animals. In all of the park there are only 37 species of mammals, from tiny mouse and shrew to caribou, moose, wolf and grizzly, and few are present in really large numbers. The same simplicity that makes the food chain easily examined makes it extremely vulnerable. Any break in it can do great or irreparable damage to the whole system. Indeed, this is why tundra is so often described as a fragile realm.

Walk on the tundra, and you will see at once what sets it apart. The few trees you encounter are small; you are above timberline, which in Denali begins between 2,500 and 3,000 feet. (Farther south timberline starts much higher—at about 10,000 feet in the Rockies—but Denali's subarctic location inhibits tree growth at relatively low altitudes.) Most trees here stand no higher than a moose; others lie low or hug the ground. More than 20 species of willow grow here—yet none approaches the size of the weeping willow commonly found along the eastern seaboard of the United States. Birch comes up to a man's waist; dogwood crouches at his heel. The prostrate posture of many tundra shrubs is an adaptation; were they to stand taller, they would be exposed to the full fury of the dry, frigid air that sweeps down from the Arctic in winter. As added protection they collect enough snow in their tangle of branches to cover them with a thick blanket that protects them not only from freezing but from drying out. Their size is no indication of their age; some of the smallest shrubs are among the oldest. Several individual willows have endured for a century or more. Most of these shrubs lie underground in shallow root systems that spread horizontally, some reaching out 10 to 15 feet.

Pushing through the brush, the visitor finds himself on a carpet of smaller tundra plants. Since he stands taller than everything that grows around him, the sense of so much open space is somewhat startling; the broad land and the high sky are almost more than the eyes can take in. One looks automatically to the ground, as though to anchor oneself to it. Here are clumps of grasses and sedges, patches of lichens and mosses and a wide assortment of flowering plants, including some that yield tart berries, provender for birds and mammals, especially for the grizzly—the greatest berry eater of them all. When dry this part of the tundra crackles underfoot and gives off a spicy smell. Tonight, however, it has gorged on rain; the mosses have turned fresh green and the lichens are slippery with the water they have soaked up.

Towering Mount McKinley, whose ancient Athabascan Indian name of Denali—"Great One"—gives the park its name, dominates the lofty mountains and ice-blue glaciers of the Alaska Range in the lower portion of this map of Denali National Park and Preserve. A single meandering road and the Alaska Railroad connect the park (blue area on inset map) with the outside world. Many-branched streams run through the 8,900-square-mile park, whose boundaries are indicated by solid red lines. Dotted red lines indicate designated wilderness areas and are coterminous with the old borders of Mount McKinley National Park, Denali's predecessor.

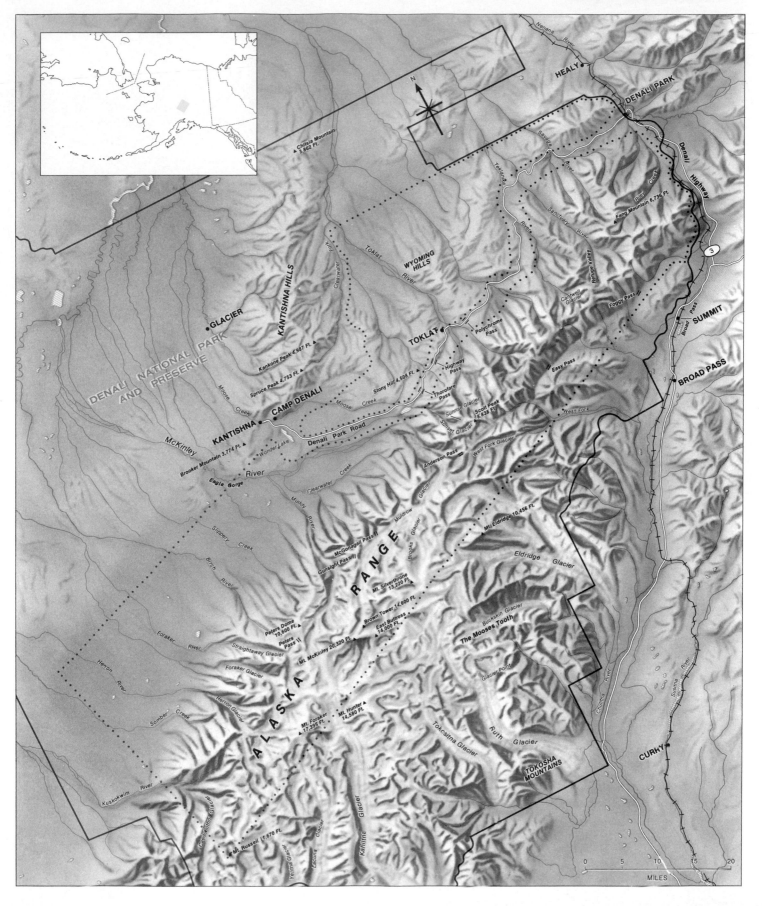

Nenans River

HEALY

DENALI PARK

Denali Highway

3

SUMMIT

BROAD PASS

Chitsia Mountain 3,862 Ft.

Broad Pass

Sawtee River

Teklanika River

Riley Creek

Fang Mountain 6,736 Ft.

Sanctuary River

Refuge Valley

Cantwell Glacier

Foggy Pass

GLACIER

KANTISHNA HILLS

Clearwater Fork

Toklat River

WYOMING HILLS

DENALI NATIONAL PARK AND PRESERVE

Kankone Peak 4,987 Ft.

TOKLAT

Polychrome Pass

Spruce Peak 4,753 Ft.

Easy Pass

Stony Hill 4,508 Ft.

Highway Pass

CAMP DENALI

Moose Creek

Thorofare Pass

Sunrise Glacier

Scott Peak 8,836 Ft.

West Fork

KANTISHNA

Denali Park Road

Sunset Glacier

McKinley

Brooker Mountain 3,774 Ft.

Wonder Lake

West Fork Glacier

Eagle Gorge

River

Clearwater Creek

Anderson Pass

Slippery Creek

Muddy River

Muldrow Glacier

Mt. Eldridge 10,456 Ft.

Birch River

R A N G E

Brooks Glacier

Eldridge Glacier

McGonagall Pass

Gunsight Pass

Mt. Silverthrone 13,220 Ft.

Buckskin Glacier

The Mooses Tooth

Foraker River

Peters Dome 10,600 Ft.

Brown Tower 14,600 Ft.

Peters Pass

East Buttress 14,000 Ft.

Glacier Point

Straightaway Glacier

Mt. McKinley 20,320 Ft.

A L A S K A

Foraker Glacier

Ruth Glacier

Heron River

Herron Glacier

Mt. Foraker 17,395 Ft.

Mt. Hunter 14,580 Ft.

Tokositna Glacier

Somber Creek

Tokositna Glacier

TOKOSHA MOUNTAINS

Chulitna River

Susitna River

CURRY

Kuskokwim River

Kanderlottna Glacier

Yentna Glacier

Lacuna Glacier

Kahiltna Glacier

Mt. Russell 11,670 Ft.

0   5   10   15   20

MILES

Tundra plants must be opportunists to survive, and as exploiters the rootless lichens clearly have the edge. They are at home clinging to twigs or bare rocks; some can even live unaffixed and blown about by the wind. Evidently lichens begin to grow earlier than other plants in winter's aftermath; a little moisture and surface warmth is all that is needed to start them off. And they take advantage of the least drop of rain, absorbing it directly into their cells without needing to wait until moisture has seeped into the ground and then traveled up through a root to the plant. They are able to lie dormant through droughts and cold spells. Moreover, they are blessed with a kind of immortality (some of the lichens in Greenland are estimated to be 4,500 years old), and do not reproduce themselves in a single season or even a decade, since they are slow to mature.

More complex structurally than the lichens, the flowering plants of the tundra are also more vulnerable. The soil from which their roots must draw sustenance is meager, largely because the cold inhibits the decomposition of rocks and organic matter into nutrients. These plants must also hang on through prolonged periods of dryness. Under such trying conditions they must reproduce in less than three months. Even in June a sudden frost may injure or kill many seed-producing flowers. A prolonged cold spell, which can happen even in summer, may do damage of another kind, preventing flies, bumblebees, butterflies and other insects from making their rounds of plants that require insect pollination to develop fertile seeds. In some years there is no seed production at all on the tundra. But the plants are prepared for this. Most of them are perennials, coming up year after year; they do not have to start life over again every spring as annuals do. Many other plants are able to reproduce asexually—without seeds. Those that have creeping root stocks or the subterranean stems called rhizomes send up leafy shoots that become individual plants; others that grow from bulbs generate bulbils, little bulbs; still others throw runners across the ground that take root where they touch.

When seeds do form and ripen, they are of a most hardy variety, armored in a thick seedcase. Seeds of arctic lupine, estimated to be 10,000 years old, were uncovered in the frozen burrow of a collared lemming deep in the tundra permafrost of Canada's Yukon Territory, on Alaska's eastern border. They proved viable even after 12 years of storage in a dry, heated room. Six sprouted a couple of days after they were placed on wet filter paper. Perhaps buried and preserved elsewhere in permafrost are the seeds or spores of species believed to have died out long ago; perhaps they will reappear. Botanists believe some arctic plants may thus have been able to weather periods of glaciation and re-establish themselves in their old habitats when the glaciers melted.

For all their ability to withstand prolonged freezing, tundra seeds need the same high temperatures—68° F. or more—to germinate that plants in warmer regions require. But once they sprout, tundra seedlings have precious little time to send down a few roots, put out a few leaves and manufacture food for next year's growth. The miracle is that many not only manage this, but also survive the winter. The purple mountain saxifrage has evolved so that it does not even have to develop leaves until its second season.

Most species of flowering tundra plants grow low, hugging the ground. Some grow in cushions or rosettes; some sprawl; some poke their flowers, though not always their leaves, a few inches above ground, ensuring that the seeds will be widely distributed by the wind. Most flowers are small; a few are so minuscule that a bouquet of their blossoms would not fill a thimble.

For all their apparent fragility, the plants are remarkably tough. Many have thick skins or fuzzy stems and leaves; the tiny hairs guard against loss of valuable moisture, and also serve to trap the sun's heat. The arctic poppy, one of the most delicate-looking of tundra plants, with its long, spindly stems and its limp yellow petals, is actually among the hardiest. It thrives on rockslides and even in the worst of tundra environments, the dry, windswept crests from which the snow is blown away in the winter.

Although there are at least 424 species of flowering plants in Denali park, each differing from the others in the way it has adapted, they share several important attributes. They are all quick-growing plants that can draw nourishment from sun and soil in temperatures that are often only slightly above freezing—a condition that would slow down or kill plants elsewhere. Actually, they get some help from the warmer microclimates at ground level, where they are protected from the full blast of cold winds. Here, too, the sun may heat up the top layer of soil and the covering mantle of vegetation, raising the temperature 20 to 30 degrees higher than that of the air just a few inches above the plants. The flowers themselves absorb the sun's rays, and their petals may register temperatures six degrees warmer than the surrounding air.

Even with the benefit of relatively warm microclimates the plants must still accommodate themselves to the brevity of the growing season, shorter in some years than others. Most give themselves a head start on next spring's growth. Before becoming dormant at summer's end, they produce a new shoot and a flower bud that lie close beneath the surface of the soil and may even poke through it under the snow. At the first touch of spring the following year the shoots take off with such speed that growth may outstrip their ability to produce food. But again the plants are prepared for this contingency: stored in their roots or rhizomes or bulbs are carbohydrates and other nutrients. The plants stand little danger of using up these food reserves before new supplies are manufactured; because of their size they require relatively small amounts of energy for maintenance. Like such plants as sunflowers, familiar farther south, some tundra plants erect hollow stems that can grow faster than those with pithy centers because they require relatively little tissue. This hollow construction creates a kind of greenhouse effect that helps ward off cold by letting the warmth of the sun enter the stem's empty core through its thin skin; heat builds up inside the core—where the temperature may be 36 degrees higher than outside—and promotes growth from within.

Spread in a mottled mat over the tundra, the plants make insect and animal life possible. Without this carpet to insulate it from direct sunlight, the permafrost that lies less than two feet below the surface in some sections of the park would melt, and dryness would eventually prevail, starving or driving away most of the species of mammals that either depend directly on the plants for food or feed on the plant eaters. The animals that tend to be most numerous in the park are also those that live closest to the plants themselves—the mouselike voles and lemmings. Seven different species of these little rodents dwell under the moss and grass in small tunnels and nests. In winter, when snow roofs their snug world, they do not hibernate but remain active.

Among them are the northern red-backed vole, which is so fond of blueberries that its teeth become stained blue during the berry season, and the haymouse, or singing vole—so called because of its continuous chirping. This industrious creature spends its summer days making hay for winter food. Adolph Murie, a naturalist who has observed the park's wildlife intensively, kept coming across caches of dried vegetation, some bushel-sized, obviously amassed by some animal. For a time he did not know what animal, but then he discovered that they were the painstaking work of this little vole, barely six inches long, tail included. Later Murie found that it also labored to store roots in holes in the ground, doing so with a kind of compulsive neatness. " The black, round nutlike tubers of the horsetail were in one pile," Murie reported, "colts-foot underground stems in another, and carrotlike roots of a pedicularis in still another."

The vole and lemming populations fluctuate cyclically, rising to a peak every three to four years, then suddenly dwindling. Since these rodents are too small to wander far afield in search of food, they must live and breed within a restricted locale. They are fecund creatures; a single female lemming may bear 20 to 30 offspring a year. This frantic reproductive pace helps offset the beating they take from the elements; for one thing, they have a surprisingly low tolerance for cold. At times, lemmings and voles become so numerous that they are dangerously close to eating themselves out of house and home; then, in the nick of time, their numbers drop. No one is sure how or why this happens. One theory suggests that, as the population gets out of hand, the animals suffer mounting social stress from overcrowding, which upsets hor-monal balance and inhibits breeding. Many of the rodents, starving and diseased, die off. The few survivors form a nucleus of breeding stock; in the meantime, the vegetation has a chance to recover. But such crea-tures as the owl, hawk, fox, weasel and marten, which depend upon voles and lemmings for food, lose this major source of supply when the rodents die, and soon their own numbers shrink.

Like voles and lemmings, snowshoe hares—named for their outsized hind feet, which actually do help them run over the snow—also suffer near-catastrophic fluctuations of their population. The snowshoe hare, found in the low-lying spruce forests and brush country of Denali park, spends a great deal of its life out in the open where it nibbles on buds, twigs and leaves in summer and on the bark of alders, willows and birches in winter. During the brief months of summer sunshine, the coat of the snowshoe hare is a grayish brown that blends in with the sur-roundings; as the days shorten and snow falls, this dun coat is replaced by a resplendent white one. The winter fur is thick and warm; its hairs contain hollow spaces that act, like the airspaces in a down-filled parka, as insulation. So well bundled is the snowshoe hare that it can tolerate temperatures as low as -70° F.

As their population climbs, the hares meet increasing competition for food. In what may be a desperate instinctive attempt to control their numbers, they take to running in groups over the snow, and thus become easy targets for such predators as the lynx, fox and owl. But these suicide runs relieve the situation only temporarily, and eventu-

An array of June flowers—chiefly white anemones and red dwarf alpine rhododendron—blooms amid patches of snow on the floor

of an upland valley in Denali park. The peaks in the background, part of the Alaska Range, reach altitudes up to 10,000 feet.

ally the hares succumb to starvation, disease and other consequences of crowding. The great die-off occurs about every 10 years, and the land that until then seemed alive with the hares' darting shapes is suddenly still and empty.

The snowshoe hare's chief foe is the lynx, a three-and-a-half-foot-long cat that likes nothing better to eat than the hare's white flesh. Immobile and camouflaged in the snow, the hare is hard for the lynx to spot; often the cat may make sudden leaps to get the hare to bolt and give its position away. If the leaps evoke no response, the lynx crouches low. This sometimes arouses the hare's curiosity and causes it to unfreeze and sit up. Then, in a flash, the lynx pounces, and the hare is no more. Lynxes pay a heavy price for their dependence on the snowshoe hare. Their own numbers rise as the hare population climbs. When the die-off of hares occurs, the lynxes are bereft of their favorite food. For a while they may get by on a diet of ptarmigan, ground squirrels and mice, and even other lynxes; but eventually they must go the way of the hare, victims of mass starvation and disease, fed on by scavengers, including ravens, foxes and grizzlies.

The drama of competing needs, played out with claw and fang on the tundra and in neighboring spruce forests, has driven some of the smaller plant-eating animals to the relative safety of rocky slopes and rock outcroppings in the park. Here they cannot be so easily dug out by bears and foxes, or set upon by lynx and wolf. The collared pika, a distant relative of the snowshoe hare, often dwells in rock piles where it caches almost everything edible within range of its home. Like many other animals, it has a craving for the salts and minerals it can get from licking and chewing pebbles. Adolph Murie watched a pika gnaw on a large pebble, which he later pocketed—and then thought twice about and returned. Gray and brown, six to seven inches long, the pika is difficult to spot among the rocks, but it may give its presence away with its alarm cry, a loud nasal "yank." It sometimes shares its habitat with the gray-and-white hoary marmot, which has black feet and a black patch across its nose, weighs 14 to 16 pounds and bears a resemblance to the woodchuck. This creature's alarm call is quite different from that of its fellow rock dweller. At the sight or sound of anything unfamiliar, it lets out a piercing whistle that serves as a clearly audible danger signal not only to fellow marmots but to many other animals as well, including the Dall sheep.

A sharp "sik-sik" is the alarm call of the arctic ground, or parka, squirrel (pronounced "parky" by Alaskans and so named because its pelts are used to make parkas). Other squirrels invariably pick up the call and repeat it, scampering into their burrows, tails flicking. Although skittish in its behavior, the ground squirrel soon grows used to human beings and ever bolder in its forays into campsites. As one danced about my boots, I found it even friendlier than the New York City Central Park gray squirrel, but my liking for its charming ways faded when one of them chewed undarnable holes in a pair of wool socks I had left at the entrance to my tent.

Quite a few of the birds and mammals at Denali park find the ground squirrel good, and even preferred, eating. It supplies an estimated 90 per cent of the golden eagle's nourishment; it is an important item in the diet of the gyrfalcon, a large graceful arctic hawk; at times, it makes up 50 per cent of the food eaten by the fox. The grizzly also relishes it; too ponderous to be an effective predator of the far swifter caribou, moose and Dall sheep, the big bear hunts down ground squirrels in their burrows. But inside its hideaway, which is furnished with several entrances, the squirrel is reasonably safe. Digging it out can be more work for the grizzly than a meal of squirrel may be worth; there is no guarantee that the dig will be successful. A cheeky ground squirrel may even dart out of one entrance and watch the frustrated grizzly, too weak-eyed to spot its small prey a few feet away, excavating an ever-widening pit at another entrance.

During winter, the ground squirrel is one of the few animals in the park that really hibernates; the grizzly, which most of us associate with hibernating, in fact does no more than fall into a deep sleep. The squirrel, curled up in its burrow, is dead to the world; it can be lifted without waking. Its temperature hovers only a few degrees above freezing, its respiration is so slow it seems not to be breathing at all, and its heartbeat drops amazingly—from a normal rate of 200 to 400 beats a minute to a rate of from five to 10. Its disappearance for six months of the year brings hardship to many of the predators that feed on it during the summer, and most of them lose weight.

In contrast to the smaller meat eaters and their prey, the large herbivores have a relatively easy life. The moose, the caribou and the Dall sheep occupy their own niches in the park's biological community, and rarely compete for food. The moose browse on branches in the woods and brushy areas they inhabit. The caribou, after wintering in the forests, summer on the tundra and in alpine pastures where they feed on lichens and assorted plants and shrubs. The sheep dwell high in the mountains and subsist there on grasses and other plants such as *Dryas*.

In the spring, the park's 1,200 or so caribou leave their wintering grounds in the forested northern and western areas and move south across the Alaska Range. In July, August and September they migrate back toward their wintering grounds. In all seasons they feed as they go, rarely pausing, snatching bites here and there; they have been aptly likened to commuters eating breakfast on the run. Using their highly sensitive noses, caribou easily find food under the snow, digging it out with their front feet; the name caribou may, in fact, be derived from *xalibu,* the Micmac Indian word for "the animal that paws through snow for its food."

The ceaseless migrations of the caribou keep them from damaging the vegetation, especially the white many-branched lichens that are their winter staple. Since these lichens grow at the rate of about one sixteenth of an inch a year, they obviously cannot stand heavy grazing. In the western coastal parts of Alaska, the lichens were largely consumed by grazing reindeer, the caribou of the Old World, which were introduced from Siberia in the 1890s to provide Eskimos with a dependable meat supply and a possible way of making a living through the sale of meat and hides. The reindeer flourished. But instead of being herded and moved back and forth from winter ranges to summer ranges—the reindeer's way of life under the nomadic Lapps of Scandinavia, for example—the animals imported into Alaska were allowed to stay on the same range all year round, and they overgrazed the lichen. Since the lichens preferred by reindeer and caribou take 50 to 100 years—sometimes longer—to regenerate, there was no chance for the range to recover quickly. During the 1930s and 1940s, the reindeer died by the thousands. There are still some 30,000 reindeer left in Alaska, compared with about 10 times that many caribou.

During their migrations within Denali park, the caribou seem to be everywhere. Sometimes bands of them join to form large herds. There are few sights more impressive anywhere than these herds streaming over the wide land, their movements accompanied by an eerie clicking that may be caused by the flexing of their leg tendons. Both sexes carry antlers; though no two pairs are alike, the male's are bigger, and the upright tines of some look like wildly gesticulating hands at the ends of long, skinny arms.

Beautiful to watch in large groups, individual caribou are somewhat ungainly. They have disproportionately big feet, averaging four by four inches; from a distance the animals look as if they are wearing overshoes. They move with their heads thrust awkwardly down and forward. But for all their apparent clumsiness, caribou are extremely capable animals. They can swim four to five miles an hour, and can gallop 30 to 40 miles an hour on snow or the soft ground of the tundra, supported by their large hoofs.

In the summer the caribou are tormented by insects. At times the animals are so harassed they cannot rest or eat, and grow weak and emaciated. The two worst pests are the parasitic warble fly and the nostril fly. The warble fly resembles a bumblebee, but neither bites nor stings; instead it lives part of its life as a larval parasite in the caribou. The fly lays its eggs on the animal's legs. The eggs hatch in about seven days; the larvae pierce the caribou's skin and travel under the hide to its back, where they cut holes in the hide through which they take in air. There they stay for weeks, emerging in May or June, when they are as big as the outer joint of a man's thumb. The warble fly's life cycle continues on the ground, where it lives through its month-long pupal stage before taking wing as an adult. Incredibly, it is not the larvae poking holes in the skin of its back that bothers a caribou so much as the persistent buzzing clouds of adult females trying to lay their eggs on its legs. A caribou under this sort of attack stiffens, points its muzzle down, shakes its head and stamps its hoofs—and may simply bolt as if in panic. Some move to breezy heights; others retreat to stand belly-deep in ponds. But escape is never really possible; nine out of 10 caribou are infested by warble flies.

The black nostril fly also resembles a bee. The female deposits the larvae in the caribou's nostrils. These work their way back to the throat, where they develop slowly over the winter; then, in March, they begin to grow rapidly. About one caribou in five may carry anywhere from 10 to 40 larvae, although as many as 156 have been taken from the throat of one animal. As the larvae come to maturity, the caribou sniff and cough and raise and lower their heads in an attempt to dislodge them. In May the larvae fall to the ground and, after a month as pupae, are ready to start the cycle over again. To escape the persistent female nostril fly, the caribou often press their noses firmly to the ground or bury them in clumps of sedge or grass.

High above the bands of beleaguered caribou, in a windy realm of their own, live the white Dall sheep. So secure are they in their mountain fastness that they apparently have no need for sharp senses of smell and hearing to alert them to danger. In- (continued on page 126)

Curling horns frame the face of a Dall ram.

Denali's Handsome Mountain Sheep

The Dall sheep that roam the high ridges of Denali Park and other mountainous parts of Alaska and Canada are the only white wild sheep in North America—and are among the handsomest animals anywhere. Their snowy coats stand out strikingly against a green mountain meadow; their relatives, the bighorn sheep of the Canadian and the American Rockies, have coats of gray or brown. The big Alaskan rams may weigh 200 pounds and grow imposing amber-colored horns that spring upward and back from their heads in a fine sweeping curve, then curl tightly around their ears. Their eyes in certain lights are gold bronze. Graceful, sure-footed creatures, they run with astonishing speed on precipitous slopes and easily leap 12- to 15-foot chasms. Because they are so swift and agile and live at such great heights, they have few predators. Only when forced to descend from their high range by snow and ice or overgrazing do they become prey to wolves and bears.

Dall ewes, young rams and yearlings graze on lush spring grasses that already carpet a sunny mountain meadow although snow remains in the nearby shaded gully. Ewes of this Alaskan species of mountain sheep band together apart from the mature rams except during mating season in November and early December. The ewes drop their single lambs —occasionally they may give birth to twins—during May or June.

A lamb almost unbalances its mother in its attempt to get at her udder. Infant Dall sheep grow so fast—they are able to keep pace with their mothers a couple of weeks after birth— that nursing soon becomes awkward. This impatient ewe is raising a leg to step over her hungry offspring.

Horns clashing, two rams playfully get in practice for the ritual battles that frequently precede mating. When that time comes, the rivals will rear on their hind legs several yards apart and then smash into each other at full speed. The buttings continue until one ram has had enough and retires from the fray.

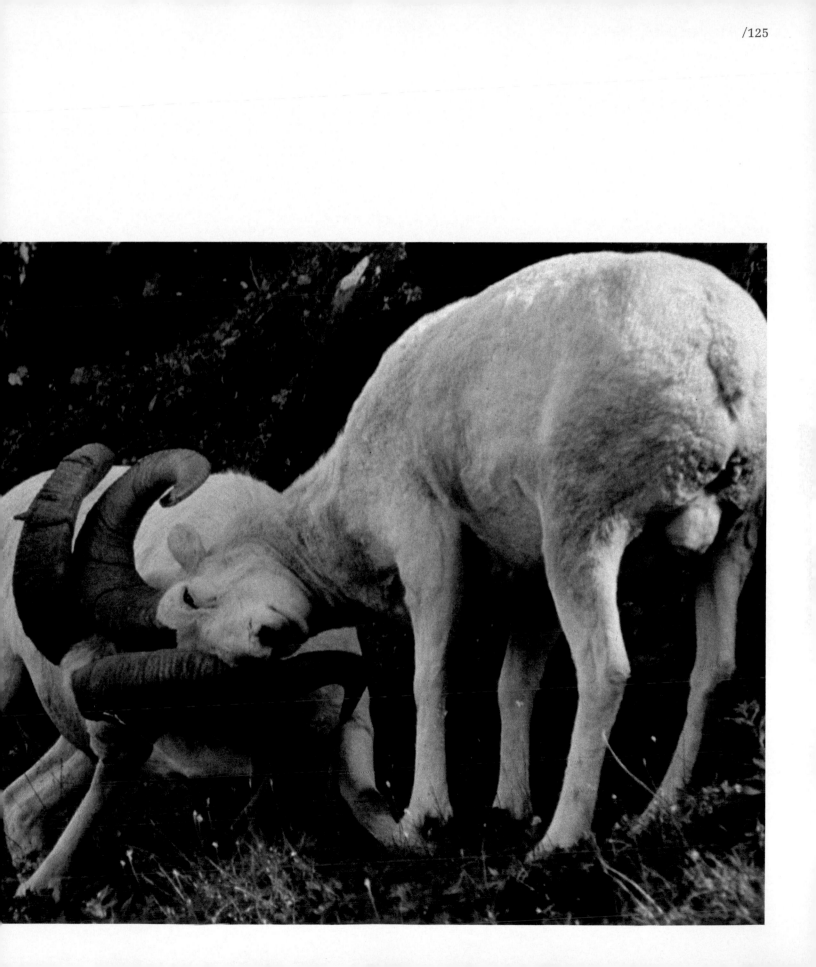

stead they rely chiefly on their eyesight, which is exceptionally keen. The male has gracefully curling horns, his age etched upon them in annual growth rings. The older he is, the more magnificent his horns. A really big ram's horns may measure about 50 inches in length, and weigh 30 pounds or more. The ram with the biggest horns usually dominates the other males. When two have horns of equal or nearly equal size, a butting contest may take place for the right to breed with the ewes. During a match, the rams come together with such a resounding crash that the impact would seem severe enough to knock the two contenders silly. However, the rams' skulls are thick and their horns sturdy, so very little damage is done.

In motion the Dall sheep is full of poised confidence. It springs about on hoofs that are soft and concave at the center to provide traction on rocks. How much at home it is on the rocks is indicated by the fact that when crossing valleys on its way from mountain to mountain, it chooses to walk on gravelly stream beds rather than on the grassy banks.

The chances of seeing Dall sheep up close are good in Denali park. Much of the population—numbering around 2,500—has little fear of man, especially in the wilderness area of the park, where hunting is forbidden. There a group of sheep can be approached within a few feet. I learned that the secret is not to alarm them by appearing to sneak up on them, but to advance slowly from downslope, standing tall. Another thrill is to follow the sheep trails. Where it is possible to walk on them at all, this is rather like traversing a steep roof, with talus slopes falling dizzily away on one side and rising precipitously on the other; but the reward is a sheep's-eye view of the tundra. It is the kind of landscape that requires a deep breath to absorb. Valleys and mountains roll everywhere toward infinity. The carpet of vegetation washes up the slopes, stopping at the point where rockslides have fallen or where the brown, tan, red and ocher soil receives the full brunt of the wind. Yet even up here, in crannies and between the rocks, grow tiny delicate flowers, including the forget-me-not, with a blossom so blue that it is like concentrated sky.

But I had reasons beyond the esthetic for following the trails of the Dall sheep. I knew that these trails were sometimes followed by wolves. They are the undisputed monarchs of this wilderness, as well as the legendary predators of all the Northern Hemisphere—preferring such large prey as Dall sheep, moose and caribou.

Everything about the wolf seems designed to encourage this formidable specialty. Wolves are big animals, and the tundra wolf of the

Alaskan interior is the largest in the world. The heaviest adult male on record weighed 120 pounds, but others have been estimated to weigh as much as 175 pounds. Sturdily built and long-legged, the wolf can not only sprint a mile or so at 25 miles an hour, but can maintain a five-mile-an-hour loose-gaited trot for hours on end. Such endurance serves it well on the hunt, especially since it most often attacks its prey on the run. The wolf's teeth enable it to rip and tear the flesh of its kill. Powerful jaws and long canine teeth allow it to fasten onto its fleeing victim and hang on. Dr. L. David Mech, author of *The Wolf*, tells of seeing one that had sunk its fangs into a moose's snout; the moose frantically lifted its attacker off the ground and swung it back and forth, but could not get free of its grip.

Since it can never be sure where its next meal will be coming from, the wolf must make efficient use of the animals it kills. Swallowing whole chunks of flesh lubricated by its saliva, it ingests enormous quantities of meat—up to 25 pounds or even more at a single feeding. In one wolf's stomach were found the liver, kidneys, windpipe, a lip, an ear and the tongue of a caribou, in addition to large pieces of its flesh and quantities of its hair. Big bones of any of the wolf's larger victims are picked clean (small animals are eaten whole); lesser bones are crunched for the marrow. Even blood that may have spilled on the ground is lapped up—in winter wolves eat the bloody snow. After feeding, the wolf rests, and digestion proceeds rapidly. A few hours later it is ready to eat again, though it may have to go several days without food before making another kill.

However swift and powerful it may be, the wolf rarely hunts alone. Since its prey is usually larger or faster, it needs help, and two or more wolves can usually accomplish what one alone could not. The basic unit of wolf society, the pack, is one of the most complex and highly developed forms of social organization in the entire animal kingdom. Parents, pups, grandparents, uncles, aunts, cousins—many generations of the same family—all live and operate together in a remarkably amiable, efficient manner, within one clearly established domain. In a study of wolves and their prey in the park, zoologist Gordon C. Haber found three major packs. One pack of around 10 operated in a territory of 500 square miles. Another of about 18 members utilized 1,000 square miles; a third pack of 10 or 15 ranged over another area of 600 or more square miles. The dividing lines between these territories were set off by scent posts—a clump of grass, an exposed root, a rock—on which the lead male and female had urinated. While my hopes of glimpsing a wolf in the park were unfulfilled, I did see some of these territorial border posts, but I have not said and will not say where since poachers could pinpoint the packs if they had such precise information.

The wolf has been called many names—including wanton killer—but a more accurate picture of its true nature has emerged from studies of its behavior in the wild. Haber and other researchers who have had a chance to observe the wolf closely now characterize it as a highly agreeable creature. Among the first to note this was Adolph Murie, whose *The Wolves of Mount McKinley,* published in 1944, is a classic in the field of natural history. During a lengthy period he spent watching a pack at its den—an enlarged fox burrow—he soon learned to recognize individual wolves by variations in their color, markings, size, shape and personality; on the basis of these quirks he gave names to some of the wolves. Robber Mask, he thought, suited a large male with a black patch of fur around his eyes. Another with "a long silvery mane and a dark mantle over the back and part way down the sides" was dubbed Dandy. This wolf commanded the respect of the others, and when he trotted off for a hunt, "his tail waved jauntily and there was a sprightly spirit in his step." The opposite of Dandy in looks and temperament was Grandpa. He seemed to be old, dragging himself about stiffy, sometimes with a limp. All the wolves got along well together, and they were solicitous of the pups born to one of the two females in the pack. The other female often behaved as if the pups were her own, playing with them and watching over them.

Life for these wolves had its regular routine. Preparatory to the hunt, the adults would assemble in the late afternoon or early evening; they always gathered with much tail wagging and frisking, as if happy to see each other. The three males would then generally go off together, accompanied sometimes by one female, and they would not return until the following day.

During the winter wolves usually travel single file through the snow, following in each other's tracks. Haber found that the wolves commonly travel along the high ridgetops—a vantage point from which they can easily spot prey and where, because the wind blows a good deal of the snow away, they have easier going. In summer, they may wander as much as 20 miles from home, completing the 40-mile round trip in from eight to 10 hours.

The wolves' summer home consists of far more than the den itself, which is basically a large hole in the ground. One den site, described by Haber, was located on a well-drained south-facing slope above a river valley, surrounded by grasses, spruces and willows. From this site the wolves had a sweeping view of the countryside. From early May to midsummer, they spent much of their time in a three-to-five-acre resting and play area situated in a forest near the den. The entire area was laced with a network of trails they had made, and near the trails were the bones of moose, Dall sheep and caribou killed by the wolves on their daily hunts and carried back to the den site in pieces. Also in the forest were wolf "beds," arranged under the spruces so as to give the resting wolves an added view of the river below—and concealment from any intruders approaching from that direction.

The den itself contained two nest chambers in which the pups were born and spent their first two or three weeks. The chambers were lined with soft underfur from the mother's coat. There were some porcupine quills lying about, left behind by porcupines that occupied the den in winter during the wolves' absence. Otherwise the den interior was clean—kept free by the mother of fecal matter, animal remains and loose dirt. When the pups were old enough to travel with the adults, the whole pack left the den area and moved on to a rendezvous site, a kind of nursery and play area where the pups remained with an adult baby-sitter while the other pack members went off on daily hunts. Often they returned from the chase with meat for the pups and the adult they left at home. They carried this meat back to the den in their big stomachs, and to obtain it the pups had only to nip and bite around the muzzles of the returning hunters to get them to regurgitate the food.

Observing their homecomings, Haber was struck by the wolves' feeling for each other. He noted: "Food brought back from a successful hunt is always ignored temporarily while the entire pack engages in an intense round of nose-rubbing, face-licking, hugging of one another with paws, romping, whining, crying, and generally ebullient display of play and affection."

The formation of strong emotional ties among wolves of the same pack is fundamental to wolf survival. An even more important guarantee of harmony—and efficiency- is the pack's strict organization. The members all have their place in the social order, led by a large, self-assured male; he is assisted by the second-ranking male in many important activities—for example, the heavy work of breaking trail in snow. The whole pack constitutes a hierarchy, and there is rarely any question of the order of ranking. The leader dominates all the others

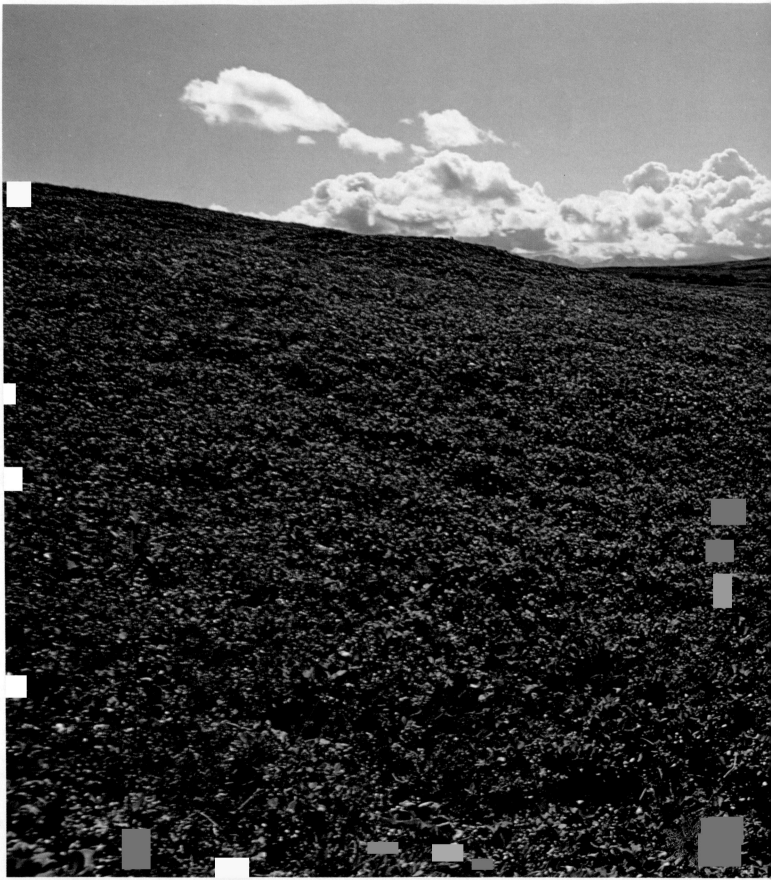

A dense, dark carpet of summertime vegetation, formed of dozens of species of low-lying plants, covers the tundra near a nameless lake

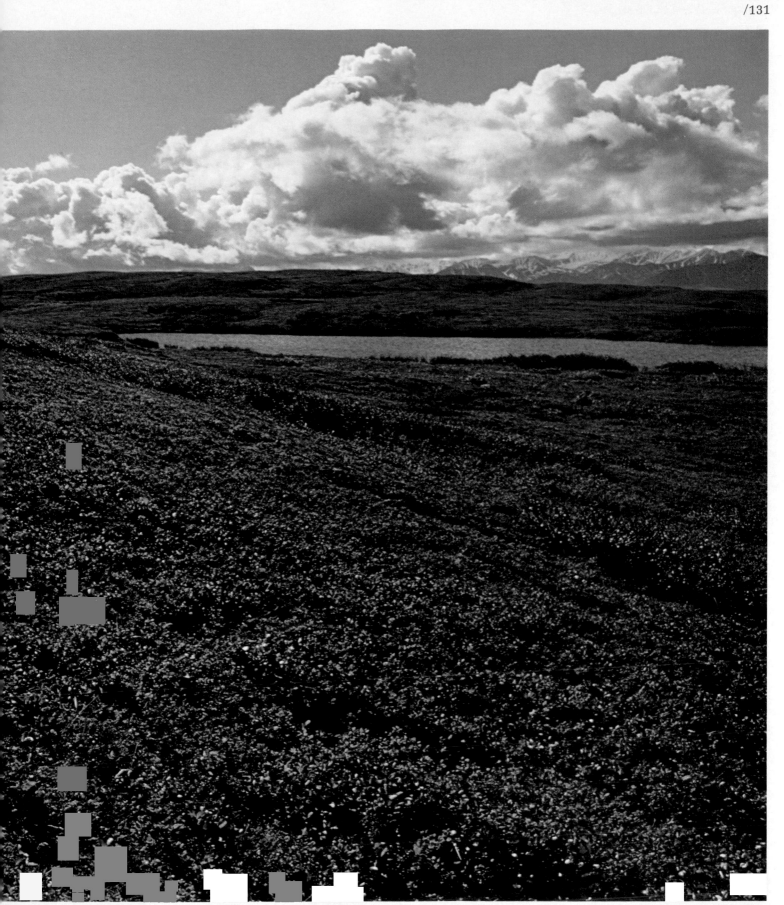

in the northern part of Denali National Park and Preserve. In the fall, most tundra plants turn from green to shades of red and brown.

physically and psychologically, his every mood coloring their moods —and he alone mates with the top-ranking female. Each wolf can and does demand submissive behavior—such as crouching—of the wolves ranked below it. But the use of naked force is rare; in more than 1,000 hours spent observing wolves in the park, Haber never witnessed a single all-out fight among the members of a pack.

On occasion the authority of the leader may be challenged by lower-ranking wolves, but only when his effectiveness as a leader has diminished as a result of age or permanent injury. But even then he may succeed in holding on to his authority if he remains aggressive and circumstances favor him. Haber observed three instances in which an injured top-ranking male managed to retain his status, perhaps because he was still very much in his prime at the time of his injury. Moreover, his disability was temporary and did not coincide with any critical moment in the life of the pack, such as courtship and mating, which might have incited challenges to his authority.

In their social behavior wolves have many ways of expressing themselves. Their tails operate as a kind of semaphore. Raised high, the tail signals dominance; lowered, it indicates submission—and the lowest-ranking wolf tucks its tail dolefully between its hind legs. Friendliness, as with dogs, involves tail-wagging, and aggressiveness is manifested by a quick switching back and forth of the whole tail or its tip. The wolf's expressive face is another indicator of mood. Under challenge a wolf asserts dominance by baring its teeth, wrinkling its forehead and holding its ears erect and forward. A wolf responding to this aggressive display shows peaceful intent by keeping its mouth shut and its brow smooth, and by pulling back its ears until they virtually touch the head. At times a dominant wolf need do no more than stare intently at a subordinate to get it to fawn in submission.

Wolves also communicate vocally. They howl, of course, but they also whimper, growl and bark. The whimpering of adults, especially in company with pups, seems to indicate solicitude; it serves also as a friendly greeting between adults. Growling means just the opposite. Barking is another way of expressing aggression, but it is also used to warn the pack of danger. Howling apparently helps to bring the pack together after a chase. It may also be used to advertise the pack's territory, or to keep another pack from trespassing, or just for enjoyment. Wolves love a good howl.

Before a howling party starts, the pack members wag their tails and whine. Then one starts to howl, pointing its muzzle skyward. The low, mournful moan that pours from its throat is one of the most stirring and beautiful of all wilderness sounds—the real cry of the wild. The howl may last from one to 10 or 15 seconds. Then another wolf joins in, and another, until the whole pack is howling.

Lois Crisler, author of *Arctic Wild,* reared two litters of wolf pups while living in the Brooks Range and not only had plenty of opportunity to listen to wolves howling, but taught herself how to howl. She describes the way one female wolf went about it: "Sometimes she ululated, drawing her tongue up and down in her mouth like a trombone slide. Sometimes on a long note she held the tip of her tongue curled against the roof of her mouth. She shaped her notes with her cheeks, holding the sound in with them for horn notes. She must have had pleasure and sensitiveness about her song for if I [howled] on her note she instantly shifted by a note or two; wolves avoid unison singing; they like chords."

As Crisler discovered, wolves make surprisingly loving pets—although many who admire wolves as wild animals would disapprove of domesticating them; they belong in the wilderness, not in the backyard. Still, those who have raised wolves in captivity have found them to be even more affectionate than dogs. There are even reports of wolves in captivity stealing puppies, kittens and baby rabbits, among others—not to harm or eat but to cuddle and care for them. Adolph Murie once took a week-old female wolf from a den to study. To obtain the pup, Murie had to climb down into the den and remove her from a litter of six. The parents did not defend the litter but stood a short distance from the den, barking and howling, obviously agitated. These predators are surprisingly docile when they are around humans, perhaps because they fear them as predators who are superior to themselves. When wounded or caught in a trap, a wolf may wag its tail and whine at the approach of the hunter or trapper.

When they are the hunters instead of the victims, however, wolves behave in an astonishingly cool and intelligent fashion. After spotting their quarry, the wolves become excited, yet manage to restrain themselves. Switching their tails back and forth and peering intently ahead, they approach the prey. When they come within attacking range of it, they often stop to study it for a few seconds, then suddenly rush at it, barking and howling. If the quarry runs, they give chase, but as soon as they find themselves being outdistanced—often after only a few hundred yards of running—they give up. If the prey holds its ground, as a moose may, the wolves look it over carefully to see whether it has any weaknesses that might make it a less formidable adversary. Wolves can detect even the most minor ailments and injuries; they look for such indications as a head held lower than normal, or a slow reflex. Often a couple of minutes are enough to tell the wolves whether to attack or not. Only when they are absolutely sure of bringing their prey down do they close in.

The precise nature of the attack varies according to the kind of prey. In the case of smaller animals like the caribou and Dall sheep, the wolves leap at the rump, belly or throat—any vulnerable part—and quickly bowl the beast over. With the moose, they must display more caution and finesse. The moose is large and powerful. Though it can outrun a wolf, it will often stand firm. An angry moose can kick its attacker 10 to 15 feet into the air. Faced with such an impressive foe, the wolves' technique generally is to go for the hind legs and nose first, taking special care to avoid the quick, deadly front hoofs. Knowing that wounded prey can be dangerous, they may wait to make the kill until their victim has grown weak from the loss of blood.

Yet for all their seeming prowess, wolves have a surprisingly low rate of hunting success. Over a 64-day period spent observing wolves during the winter, Haber recorded all the activities—hunting and scavenging— of one pack of 13 wolves in the park. They ate 16 carcasses of various animals killed by winter cold during this period; but of 113 live moose they encountered and tested, the wolves managed to kill only 10. During the same period 224 Dall sheep were chased by the wolves but only 13 were caught, and of 26 caribou pursued only one was killed. "The animals the wolves got had some handicap," Haber reported, "and although it is difficult to ascertain the condition of those that escaped, it can be assumed that they were generally the fittest."

Keeping their population in balance with the available food supply is most critical to the survival of the wolves. Several natural controls seem to be at work here. For one thing, the boundaries between the packs— boundaries the wolves usually respect—help limit the numbers of wolves in any one territory at any one time. Moreover, wolves restrict mating, which is almost always the exclusive prerogative of the top-ranking male and female. Both curb the tendencies of the other pack members in this direction; the male polices the lower males, the female the lesser females.

But mating time can generate problems. In one pack that Haber followed in late February and the first half of March, the wolf breeding season in the park, the leader and the second-ranking male both appeared eager to mate with the top-ranking female. She, for her part, seemed to prefer the second male, and he made repeated attempts to approach her. But the leader would have none of it. With what Haber described as "unmistakable yet by no means vicious displays of dominance," the top wolf managed to keep his competitor in an almost constant state of submission and retained the female for himself. There was no more trouble. On the contrary, after the pair mated, the unrequited suitor assumed what Haber called the role of a "vicarious husband," being especially attentive to the female before her pups were born, and later helping to care for them as if he had fathered them.

Besides restricted mating and territoriality, other factors may be at work in population control. Haber discovered that the packs occupied roughly the same areas—and had maintained basically the same populations—as they had several decades before, when Murie first began studying their behavior, and that the distribution of their prey had also remained remarkably similar to what it was then. The wolves even used many of the same dens and travel routes. But this type of balance can fluctuate—within limits. If the numbers of available prey animals—that is, those the wolves can easily and safely kill—increase, the wolf population grows slightly. On the other hand, if the prey population declines, wolf numbers seem to shrink somewhat—and not just by coincidence. In hard times, when a pack has grown too numerous for its own good, the bonds between the high- and low-ranking members seem to weaken. Higher-ranking wolves show less concern for the weaker—often younger—lower ranks. Those that find it difficult to keep up with the pack during the arduous winter are simply left to perish. Conversely, when the pack is below the size that the available food supply can support over a long period, high-ranking members seem to care more about what happens to the weaker members, thereby improving their chances of survival. According to Haber, this would suggest that "some sort of dynamic balance has been achieved, the wolves and their prey having established a condition of mutual adaptation to each other."

Wolves close in on a bull moose at bay.

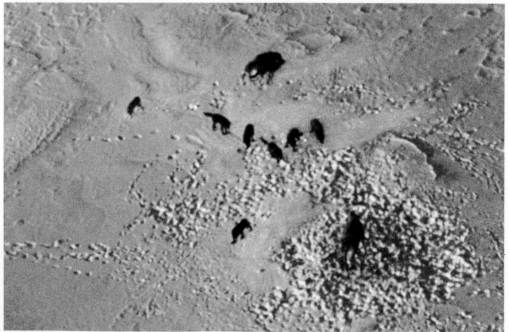

Deciding not to attack, the pack breaks off the hunt.

The pack circles the prey, sizing him up.

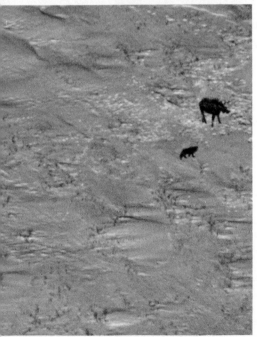

The wolves retreat in search of weaker prey.

The Wolves— a Hunting Society

The most exciting—and most elusive—among Denali park's animals are its wolves. They number more than 50, most of them grouped into one of several packs. One of the packs is shown hunting in the sequence of unique aerial photographs at left and overleaf, taken by Gordon C. Haber, a zoologist who spent years studying the park's wolves and their prey. The packs roam over their own well-defined territories, each with an area of hundreds of square miles, pursuing moose, caribou and Dall sheep.

Each pack is usually made up of wolves from different generations of the same family and is led by a male that dominates the activities of the entire group. The other wolves are ranked below him in hierarchical order. The leader ordinarily relies on the second-ranking male to break trails in the snow and to assume the initiative on most hunts. But in emergencies, and when the pack has hunted too long without success, the leader will take full command—having carefully husbanded his energies for just such an occasion.

Wolves usually hunt in groups but, as the sequence at left shows, they do not always press home the attack. This pack was photographed encountering a moose, an animal wolves respect for its ability to defend itself with its large, sharp front hoofs. So formidable did this moose appear to the wolves that they decided against trying to kill it.

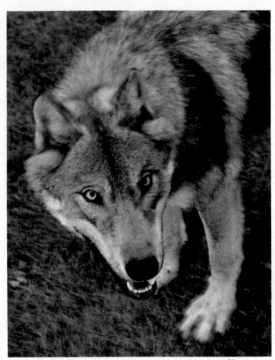

A wolf's yellow eyes express its wary intelligence.

Advancing single file, the wolves of a 13-member pack follow the trail blazer, the lighter male in front. The pack's leader, however, is the

black male fifth from the end, the only wolf to carry his tail high—a sign of his dominance. Directly in front of him is the ranking female.

5/ The Timeless Arctic

The justification for present-day exploration is almost exclusively the selfish one of giving oneself the exhilaration of that most glorious of all pastimes, setting foot where no human being has ever trod before.

ROBERT MARSHALL/ *ALASKA WILDERNESS*

Almost a third of Alaska lies north of the Arctic Circle. The Alaskan Arctic, as it is called, was until the middle of this century little disturbed by man—only a scattering of residents, mostly Eskimos and Indians, made peace with the hostile climate and the remoteness of the place. The forbidding Brooks Range sweeps from east to west across the region like a crenelated wall that only the most determined of people could breach. The plants and animals of this vast realm of snow, ice and tundra maintained a natural balance rare in the modern world. But the discovery of oil on Alaska's northern coast in 1968 ended the long isolation of the remote Arctic. Today a steady stream of aircraft flies over the mountains to and from the Prudhoe Bay oil fields, and an 800-mile-long pipeline carries an endless flow of oil south through the mountains.

Despite these intrusions, much of the Alaskan Arctic remains a wilderness largely untouched and little explored by man. Enormous sections of this timeless land have been set aside as federally protected wilderness areas, including about half of the 28,000-square-mile Arctic National Wildlife Refuge that occupies the northeastern corner of the state. Established in 1960 and greatly expanded in 1980, it is managed by the U.S. Fish and Wildlife Service and is dedicated to the preservation of arctic flora and fauna in their natural states.

The refuge and its huge neighbor to the south, the 14,000-square-mile Yukon Flats National Wildlife Refuge, are home for a variety of animals ranging from minks to musk oxen, from pikas to polar bears. One of Alaska's largest caribou herds, estimated at 120,000 members, roams the region. Millions of birds return to their nesting grounds here each summer, including terns from the Antarctic, golden plovers from South Africa and whistling swans from Chesapeake Bay. Here in nameless mountains and trackless valleys it is possible to travel for days on end without detecting any evidence of humanity and to have the kind of wilderness experiences that are largely forgotten in other parts of the world. I had such experiences on a visit to the Arctic refuge, and recorded them in a diary.

JULY 17/I flew here to Last Lake this morning with my guide, Spence Linderman, from Fort Yukon, a settlement of Kutchakutchin Indians on the Arctic Circle, 150 miles to the south. For much of the trip the landscape below was flat but intricately patterned. Meandering rivers and streams have shifted their courses so many times that the area is grooved with old dried-up beds. These are now filled with vegetation in various stages of development, standing out as light-green squiggles in the darker green of the surrounding spruce forest. Crescent-shaped lakes, known as oxbows, reflect the sky (oxbows form when a river has shortened its course, cutting off an old looping bend; the bend then becomes a lake). In treeless areas the land is a honeycomb of polygonal shapes, a result of the seasonal churning of the earth above the underlying layer of permafrost.

As we neared the Brooks Range, a broad valley opened before us, with the Sheenjek River flowing down it in silver coils. The low, bald foothills grew steadily bigger, then lifted themselves into mountains. More and more lakes came into view, and at the last lake on which a floatplane can land—hence the name Last Lake—we touched down. The pilot waited no longer than it took to unload our equipment on the shore. "See you in two weeks," he said, waved from his window and buzzed off. With the plane gone, stillness soon returned, the surface of the lake was again smooth and the mouths of hungry fish began to leave rings on it. We are now alone in the wilderness. The quiet is at once welcome and forbidding. It is the quiet of implacable nature, the quiet of things growing, the quiet of things dead.

Strangers to each other, my guide and I find ourselves suddenly linked by our humanity in a country where there are no other human beings. Spence is a lean, bearded graduate student of wildlife management at the University of Alaska. He has dared more since he came to Alaska from Kansas than most men do in their lifetimes. One winter, with a Norwegian friend, he skied across the North Slope, over the Brooks Range and down to Arctic Village, another Indian settlement southwest of here. He knows what to expect of uncompromised wilderness, and he has outfitted us well for the two weeks we will spend wandering through the heart of the wildlife refuge. Besides food—much of it freeze-dried—a tent, a small Primus stove and white gasoline for fuel, we have a life raft, a revolver and a radio beacon capable of sending out a distress signal for two hours over a radius of 150 miles.

After pitching our blue nylon tent close to the shore and caching our gear under two columnar white spruces, we shouldered our packs and took off on an exploratory hike. Almost at once we made a discovery. Deep in the grass clustered a rare moss, *Splachnum luteum*. Mosses bear no flowers, but this one was, so to speak, in full bloom. Each of its spore capsules formed a cream-colored parasol about a quarter of an inch across, held a couple of inches high on a thin red stem. Added to its curious appearance, this moss has another remarkable feature—it flourishes only on animal dung.

Beyond the grassy area was a stand of narrow white spruce, the trees 15 to 20 feet apart. They showed clear signs of their struggle to survive in the Arctic. Some leaned toward each other, the ground under them convulsed by frost action. Others had been rocked over by the wind. One that had been killed almost to its roots managed to put out a shoot, which then reared into a new tree. None of the spruces was really big, and none had a trunk more than a foot in diameter—yet almost all were probably a century or more old. Back in 1956 scientists from a number of American universities came here to study the plants and animals and counted the rings in the trunk of one tree. Their tally showed that it had been rooted to the spot for 298 years. In the short arctic summer, producing a ring of wood is the greatest luxury a plant can indulge in. Trees grow very slowly in this region. A spruce takes 30 years to reach a height of five feet, a century to grow to 20 feet.

Though it is still only July, summer already seems to be ending. On our hike today we saw evidence of this behind the stand of spruce in a hummocky meadow. Many of the tundra plants there had gone to seed. Bright green pillows of moss campion, embroidered a few weeks ago with garnet-red buds and pink flowers, lay unadorned in the grass. Withered trumpets of dwarf rhododendron *(continued on page 146)*

The vast Arctic National Wildlife Refuge covers the eastern sector of the Brooks Range and part of the North Slope, the gently inclined plain that extends to the Beaufort Sea (blue area in inset map). The refuge's boundaries, partially shown by solid red lines, enclose a region almost the size of South Carolina. Within the refuge is a 12,500-square-mile wilderness area, indicated by dotted red lines in this detail map. The 200-mile Sheenjek River, at the lower center, is one of 25 Alaskan streams designated as federally protected National Wild and Scenic Rivers.

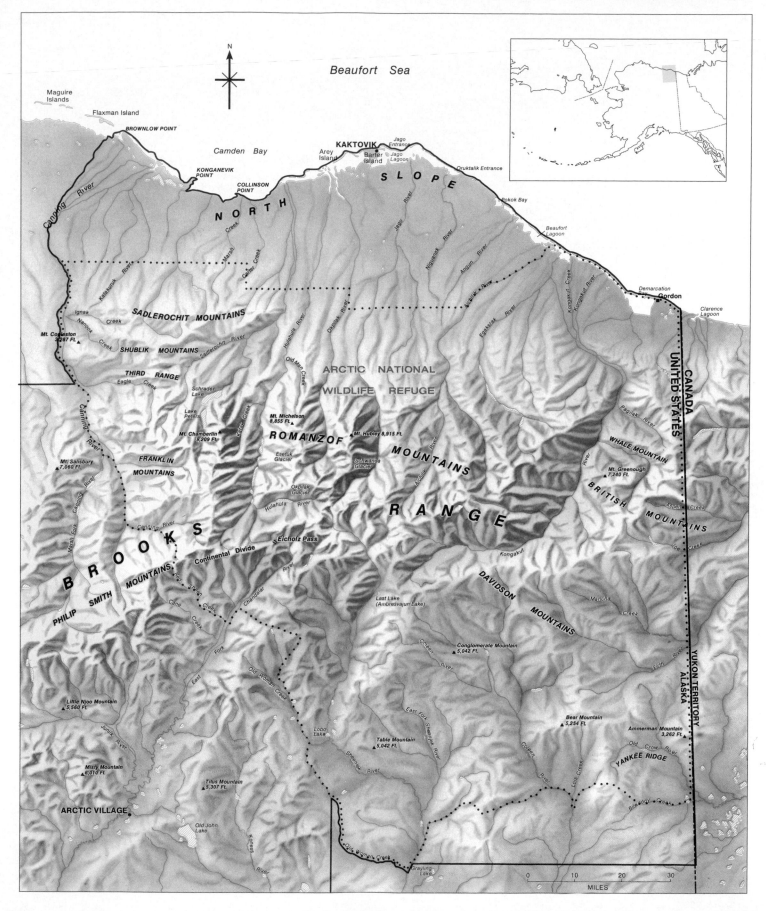

N

Beaufort Sea

Maguire
Islands

Flaxman Island

BROWNLOW POINT

Camden Bay

KONGANEVIK
POINT

COLLINSON
POINT

Arey
Island

KAKTOVIK

Jago
Entrance

Barter
Island

Jago
Lagoon

Oruktalik Entrance

Pokok Bay

N O R T H   S L O P E

Beaufort
Lagoon

Canning   River

Marsh   Creek

Carter   Creek

Jago   River

Niguanak   River

Angun   River

Aichilik   River

Demarcation
Bay   Gordon

Clarence
Lagoon

Katakturuk   River

Ignak   Creek

SADLEROCHIT   MOUNTAINS

Nanook   Creek

Mt. Copleston
3,287 Ft.

SHUBLIK   MOUNTAINS

Sadlerochit   River

Old   Man   Creek

Hulahula   River

Okpilak   River

ARCTIC   NATIONAL

WILDLIFE   REFUGE

Kongakut   River

Kongakut   River

Egaksrak   River

United States   CANADA

THIRD   RANGE

Eagle   Creek

Schrader
Lake

Lake
Peters

Mt. Chamberlin
9,209 Ft.

Katakt   Creek

Mt. Michelson
8,855 Ft.

Mt. Hubley 8,915 Ft.

ROMANZOF

MOUNTAINS

Pagilak   River

WHALE   MOUNTAIN

Mt. Greenough
7,240 Ft.

BRITISH

Mt. Salisbury
7,060 Ft.

FRANKLIN

MOUNTAINS

Esetuk
Glacier

Schwanda
Glacier

Okpilak
Glacier

Aichilik   River

R A N G E

MOUNTAINS

Canning   River

Hulahula   River

Aspen   Creek

Joe   Creek

Canning   River

Canning   River

Marsh Fork   Canning   River

B   R   O   O   K   S

SMITH   MOUNTAINS

Red   Sheep   Creek

Eicholz Pass

Continental Divide

Chandalar   River

Last Lake
(Ambresvajun Lake)

Kongakut

DAVIDSON

MOUNTAINS

Mancha
Creek

PHILIP

Cane   Creek

Fork

East   Fork

Old   Woman   Creek

Crtlean   River

East Fork Sheenjek River

Conglomerate Mountain
5,042 Ft.

Firth   River

Little Njoo Mountain
5,560 Ft.

Lobo
Lake

Sheenjek   River

Table Mountain
5,042 Ft.

Bear Mountain
5,254 Ft.

Coleen   River

Lois   Creek

Ammerman Mountain
3,262 Ft.

YUKON TERRITORY
ALASKA

Junjik   River

Misty Mountain
6,010 Ft.

Titus Mountain
5,307 Ft.

Old   Crow   River

YANKEE   RIDGE

Billwdly   Creek

ARCTIC VILLAGE

Old John
Lake

Koness   River

Old   Woman   Creek

Grayling
Lake

0   10   20   30

MILES

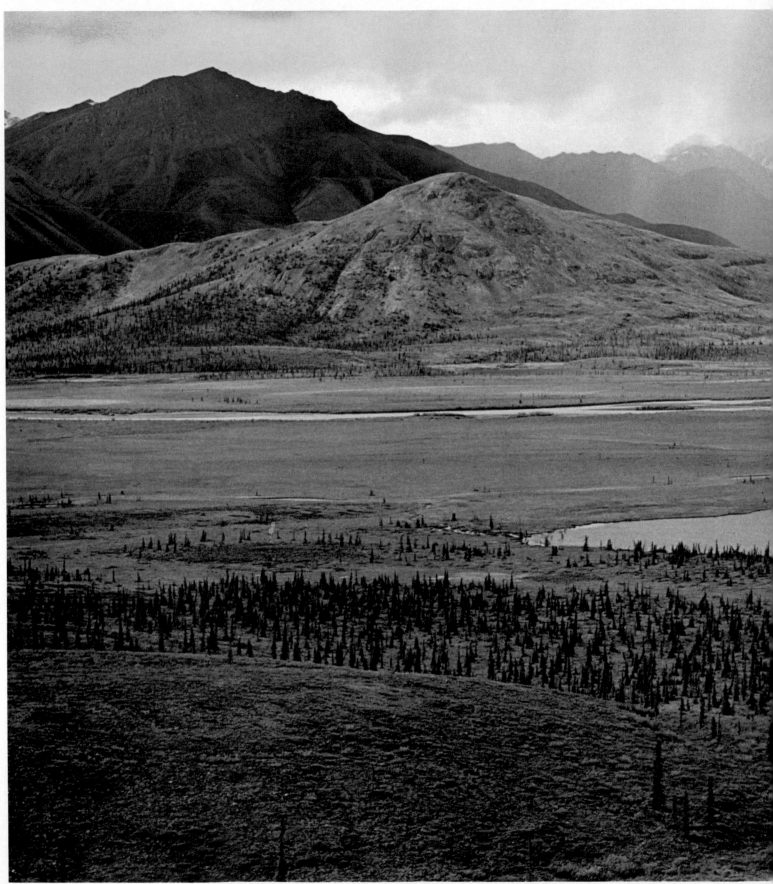

Looming above nameless mountains of the Brooks Range, a July rain squall advances toward the Sheenjek River and Last Lake. So harsh

is this arctic environment that the white spruce trees in the foreground stand only about 20 feet high—even after a century of growth.

that recently had been a bright fuchsia now hung brown on their stems; stalks of arctic lupine dangled furry pods where dark blue blossoms had been. And no birds sang. They already have finished their round of seasonal activities—proclaimed their territories, gone through their courtship displays, bred, made their nests, laid their eggs and hatched them. Now no longer in need of their voices they have lapsed into silence. A few have already flown south; others are getting ready to follow. Soon only the hardiest will be left, among them the black raven, which follows the wolves on their winter hunts, scavenging the meager leftovers of the predators' kills.

We examined some of the withered flowers, then cut through the meadow to the base of a nearby mountain, a 5,000-foot mound of frost-shattered limestone. We climbed it to a point from which we had an eagle's-eye view of the great U-shaped glacial trough that is the Sheenjek Valley. Below, like soldiers ranged upon a battlefield, stood the widely spaced spruces. Where their ranks thinned the tundra began, a sweep of vibrant green that flowed, like the river itself, between two somber rows of mountains.

The silent valley gave us a distinctly eerie feeling. It seemed deserted, as if all the animals inhabiting it had fled. We turned to inspect a shallow cave behind us. On the ledge above the cave a large empty nest protruded. It was built of sticks, probably by golden eagles, and the rocks beneath it were splashed orange by a species of lichen that thrives where bird droppings fall. But we saw no new white bird droppings that would have indicated recent occupancy of the nest. In another small cave not far away the floor was littered with porcupine scats, small, wood-colored pellets that gave off the scent of resin—the porcupine's favorite food here is the inner bark of spruce. But the pellets were dry; obviously the tenant of the cave had not lived here for some time—perhaps not since the previous winter.

Around a bend, we found ourselves above another valley, broader and seemingly even more void of animal life than the first, with distant mountains that slashed the sky like shark fins. We hiked along the slopes above the valley, aware of the utter stillness, the deep, abiding silence. When we rested, the quiet drifted down around us; when we walked, it followed us, interrupted only by the moan of the wind. It induced a sense of loneliness, but of a welcome sort. Suddenly both Spence and I felt elated. A light rain started falling, more in specks than drops, and we could have gone on without getting soaked, but we chose to turn back. We agreed that the eight miles we had covered would be enough hiking for our first day—and besides, we were thinking of the fire we would build, the food we would eat and the downy warmth of our sleeping bags.

JULY 18/Early this morning we left our raft and most of our supplies bundled up at the lake and began a five-day backpack trip along the Sheenjek and some of its tributaries—a journey that will take us into the mountains to the northwest, a region little explored by white men. Our plan is to return then to base camp, pick up our gear and finally float down the Sheenjek to Lobo Lake, where our pilot will pick us up. Not far along on our journey we came upon a "river glacier," as many Alaskans call it—not a true glacier but a broad dam of layered ice that builds up on top of shallow arctic rivers during winter. Water moving in the shoals of the river bed pushes through and over surface ice, where some of it freezes. As this process repeats itself through the winter, it builds up the ice in layers that can grow to a thickness of a yard or more. Spence says the proper term for the phenomenon is *Aufeis*, German for "overflow ice." We climbed up on it and half walked, half skidded across its slippery surface. In spots the ice was soft; when scuffed it broke into crystalline splinters about two inches long. As we scrutinized a mass of these crystals, we were startled by a loud, unexpected boom. Another boom followed a few minutes later. Curious to learn what had made this thunder, we walked in the direction of the noise and arrived at the upstream end of the *Aufeis*. A ledge of rotting ice hung over the shallow water. Exposed to the melting action of the sun and undermined from below by the current, two pieces, each three or four feet thick, had broken off the ledge in sections 25 and 50 feet long, big enough to have made the booming sounds we had heard.

We hopped onto dry land, and crunched for a while over the moss-and-lichen floor of a grove of white spruce. The first mosquitoes of the day, brought to life by the sun's warmth, came out to greet us. They whined about our heads, zoomed onto our clothes, buzzed into our mouths. Soon our backs were acrawl with them. Spence would shout, "Die, varmints!" And with a mighty swat of his broad hand he would kill the dozen or so congregated on his sleeve. There are 30 different species of mosquito in Alaska. The first to hatch come out along the Panhandle as early as January, and here in the pond-dotted Arctic they are the scourge of summer. One biologist in Anchorage insists that within two hours they can drain half the blood from a person incapacitated and exposed on the tundra.

Except to rub more insect repellent on our faces, necks and hands, we had but one option—to get used to the mosquitoes. I surprised myself by dozing off in a cloud of them after lunch and waking up less concerned about them than about other matters, specifically how we were going to get across the river. The Sheenjek, fed by melting glaciers, consists of several channels, and today these were murky with mud that had been stirred up by a local rainstorm. Since we had no inkling of how deep the channels might be, we took the precaution of fording only where they were widest and the water, we presumed, was shallowest. Even so, it was unexpectedly deep along the banks, and in some places there was an underlying layer of thick, sticky mud. The way this ooze grabbed at my boots frightened me; quicksand is common in Alaskan rivers, especially along their edges. And even after we were safely across one channel and on the bank, we had to crash through willow thickets covering the sand and gravel bars—where whole armies of mosquitoes waited to ambush us—and then had to plunge across another channel and another.

But we made it at last to the other side of the river. Once there, we faced several miles of bogs thickly sown with tussocks, wobbly mounds of matted grass, each about a foot wide and a foot high. It was impossible to walk on them—and just as impossible to walk between them because they grow so close together. The best we could do was stagger over them, trying to keep our balance, which wasn't easy with our packs. And whenever we tipped off the tussocks, our boots plunged into the stagnant water that collects around the mounds, its drainage impeded by the permafrost shield underneath.

As we were struggling along, we met a tiny brown lemming doing the same. Runoff from the recent rain had probably flooded it from its home. It was the first mammal we saw today—and, as it turned out, the last. Where are the bigger mammals? They could be hiding—yet there seem to be few places to hide in such open country as this. I keep wondering whether there has been some recent drop in the animal population in this locality that has temporarily disrupted the food chain and forced predators to go elsewhere in search of prey. If so, that lone lemming we saw could be a very important creature—one of the survivors on which the restoration of the food chain will depend.

Though we missed seeing mammals today, the beauty of the country we passed through more than made up for our disappointment. Mountains reared on either side of us, giant thrones for big, puffy clouds. The glassy light typical of the far north made every object stand out in

Two mouselike lemmings peer warily from the mouth of their burrow before venturing forth to eat fresh spring buds and shoots. These tiny, three-ounce rodents multiply in huge numbers; each female can bear as many as 20 offspring a year, causing periodic population explosions. When food runs short, the lemmings die off by the thousands.

gentle relief. Shifting cloud patterns would cause changing lights and colors. One moment the slopes would look blue, while the valley glowed bright green; next, the colors would rearrange themselves, and the slopes would turn green and the valley blue. The effect of these changes was otherworldly. Indeed, there were times today when our surroundings seemed more dreamed than real, especially when we came upon robins—common garden-variety robins—skittering over the grass while a golden eagle soared overhead on broad wings. Spence assured me that robins are no strangers to the Arctic, and that they nest in willow thickets hereabouts.

Now, as I write, I sit on the steep side of a nameless hill above a nameless tributary of the Sheenjek River. The sun has dropped behind the mountain opposite our camp, and the tent lies in cool shadow. But far off to the right, well beyond the Sheenjek, the sun's rays play on the valley like a spotlight. And where this golden path begins to narrow, a double rainbow climbs above the mountains into a deep-gray sky.

JULY 19/We have camped near the stream on a hillock above another patch of *Aufeis*. It detonates every hour or so as shelves of rotten ice crack off and slump into the water. The mountains crowd in here so that they shut out the evening sun. They are worn and jagged on top, with caves like empty eye sockets in their faces. Frightening. We feel no temptation to climb them. Below us stretches a narrow valley, a funnel for the gloom. Looking back we can see all the way to last night's campsite, 10 miles away. Considering the bogs, tussocks and rolling cobbles that lay in our path today, that is a long way to have come. But I am still a creature of speed, of cars and airplanes, as yet unaccustomed to measuring miles in terms of my own footsteps. Somehow I am disappointed that we have not come farther.

En route to this camp, we were often accompanied by brown slender-necked upland plovers, which kept flying ahead of us, coming back and flying on ahead again. And in a grove of cottonwoods, trees I hadn't expected to find this far north, we surprised a covey of willow ptarmigan —several families, with six or more chicks each. They whirred up from the ground, raucous in their alarm, then clattered down into the bushes. But of any other creatures we again had only signs—torn-up patches of tundra where a bear or wolverine had clawed for roots and grubs; clipped willow branches on which moose had fed; and countless criss-crossing caribou trails. As we followed the trails, we found ourselves being pulled forward, drawn on by the excitement of knowing that we were among the first whites to come up this valley on foot. And despite the gray desolation of the scene that confronts us now, we would not want to be any other place tonight.

JULY 20/This morning we were wakened by a red-and-white helicopter flying in low over our camp and shattering the stillness. We resented the intrusion, all the more because the chopper was probably carrying a team of oil geologists to their day's work in the mountains. Would they go home tonight to warm beds, like commuters? What can they know of this land—how can they come to love it and want to protect it—if they have not walked it? I know I am being unfair to them; I have been told that some geologists fall so much in love with the Arctic that they privately hope they will never find minerals or oil. Still, tonight we *feel* all of the 14 miles we hiked today; each mile is a part of us now, lodged in muscle as well as memory.

After breaking camp at 9 a.m., we advanced up the valley, gradually ascending beyond the last of the trees into the true Arctic—a mountainous land so windy, frigid and desiccated through much of the year that most plant life lies prostrate. Here in the open upland there is only a thin, frayed carpet of plants over the permafrost, and the lack of trees, and hence of wood, makes campfires out of the question. Yet there is a curiously benign quality to the land. Perhaps it is the green breadth of the tundra that creates this effect. Or perhaps it is the light. Today it was soft and rich, mellowing even the harshness of the mountains and decreasing their apparent distance from us. But what can the same country be like in winter, in the cold and dark, with the wind howling? I remembered what Dr. Robert B. Weeden, a wildlife biologist at the University of Alaska, once wrote: "Sometimes in the North, you think the land will never live; will never know the warmth of sun; will never ever give a reluctant nod to spring."

On a hillside, we came upon an orange metal box, just sitting there. It was a U.S. Air Force emergency kit, apparently dropped to someone in trouble. The rifle, ax, knife, food and matches listed on the outside of the box had been removed; only those things remained for which there could have been no use in winter—a gill net, a fish line, some hooks and lures. We also discovered, stuck to the bottom, a package of rusty safety pins and a booklet listing survival techniques. We stowed the fishing gear and booklet with our equipment and used the pins to fasten yesterday's still-wet socks to our packs. As we walked along, the socks swayed in the breeze—laundry hung out to dry.

Heading northwest, we climbed through a pass between two ridges to a lake as flat and gray as a pewter tray, with no frills of vegetation to soften the sharp line between water and land. Beyond the lake was an enormous arena surrounded by mountains. We sat down on the dry grass and lichens to have our lunch—a few chunks of cheese, a couple of pieces of high-energy bread with a dark molasses flavor, and some dried apricots and pears, washed down with water scooped from a tiny pool. Where the environment is so pure, you do not have to worry about contaminated water.

As we ate, we were facing north. We began talking about all the unexplored land that lay between us and the Beaufort Sea, and suddenly I felt seized by a desire to hike the 120 miles to Kaktovik, an Eskimo community on an offshore island at the edge of the Arctic refuge. Spence confessed to the same urge. It was, of course, a madly impractical idea. We would have been completely cut off from the world, for Averill Thayer, the manager of the refuge, who knew our general itinerary, would not have been aware of our change of plan. And we would have had to live off the land, since we had only two days' worth of provisions left. Spence was convinced that we would find a stray caribou to eat; I was not so sure. Slowly our euphoria subsided and we decided to stick to our original plan. Just as well: hunting game is illegal except in dire emergency.

The encircling mountains were angry looking, furrowed and beetled by the folding of the earth's crust, which had given them shape. Even so, in this vast walled-in area we felt secure and serene. After lunch we strolled across the arena to get an idea of its real size; it proved to be fully a mile wide. As we walked, dry threads of gray-white lichen snapped underfoot, and the noise scared a Baird's sandpiper, a female, that flew off to scold us from a distance. We looked for the cause of her excitement and found one of her chicks, a mottled ball of down that hugged the pebbles, then suddenly toddled off, high-legged, miniwinged, not yet able to fly. It is unusual for a chick to be born so late in the season; perhaps the mother's first clutch of eggs had been destroyed. I found it incredible that such shore birds as sandpipers should come so far inland to nest. "Not at all," said Spence, adding that the term shore birds is a misnomer. They are associated with shores only when migrating or wintering in southern regions. In the Arctic they nest inland, laying their eggs on the ground. These are so well camouflaged that they can easily go unnoticed; indeed, years passed before ornithologists could find any eggs belonging to the wandering tattler, a shore

The Caribou—
Nomads of the North

The Alaskan caribou has its own special means of coping with the harsh environment. Its dense brown-and-white coat is among the animal world's warmest. Its broad hoofs support it over treacherous terrain—boggy slopes and rocky ridges—and on soft snow. The caribou has also solved the problem of stoking its appetite in a region of sparse vegetation: it lives as a nomad.

Caribou herds ceaselessly travel between winter and summer ranges. The migrants pictured here roam over Alaska's most rigorous territory, the land above the Arctic Circle. From November through March they graze in Canadian rangeland to the southeast, where they paw through the light snow cover to expose lichens and sedges, their favorite foods. In April immense herds trek northward hundreds of miles to their summer range in the windy North Slope, where they feed on the tundra's low-growing plants. When fall approaches the herds again drift south; rutting and mating occur in October, during migration.

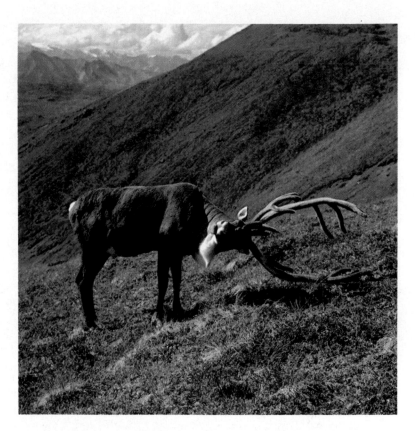

On an arctic slope a caribou bull rubs his fully grown antlers to remove their furlike covering. The female caribou also has antlers, but the bull's are bigger and are used to intimidate his rivals in contests for the females during the autumn mating season.

Caribou move across a tundra ridge, feeding as they go. These majestically antlered animals seldom pause in their wandering except to sleep, chew their cuds and drop their calves. They like high, windswept terrain in summer for the relief it offers from flies.

bird that migrates between Alaska and the California coast or the islands of the South Pacific.

After our walk we picked up our packs and started southeast, heading back in the direction of our base camp at Last Lake. Soon after setting out we discovered the entrance to a canyon where rocks rose in jagged black pinnacles. We stood for a moment, awed, then ventured in. The atmosphere was oppressive. The canyon walls descended sharply to a stream that foamed between sharp rocks, and almost the only form of vegetation flourishing here was red moss that clung in clots to the stone. The way grew progressively narrower until, to go farther, we would have had to step into the stream. We retreated to a rocky slope and began to climb it; for each step gained we seemed to slide back two. When we reached the top, breathless, hearts pounding, we turned and saw a waterfall spurting from a hole in the rocks into an inky pool. Exulting over our discovery, we thought of calling this sharp-walled cul-de-sac Hole-in-the-Wall Canyon. If we want to, we can submit the name to the state and national boards on geographical names and probably have it accepted. But we finally decided that this would be a little like scribbling on a freshly painted wall. We both felt that there ought to be a few nameless places still left in the world.

When we had caught our breath, we resumed our hike, moving along a grassy ridge through a tilted valley to our present campsite, about 18 miles from Last Lake. We dropped our packs and walked a mile or so ahead to get some idea of what lay in store for us tomorrow. In front of us reared a row of snow-striped mountains. To the right, way up high, a glacier sprawled between two peaks. Glowing softly, it looked like some giant predator asleep.

JULY 21/This morning, leaving Spence behind to take pictures of tundra vegetation, I explored a mountain stream fed by meltwater from the glacier. The way was steep, but at first the ascent was pleasant. The stream splashed down a staircase of rocks set between the slopes of a ravine, and grass padded the banks on either side. Where the grass carpet became frayed, a pair of weathered caribou antlers, still attached to part of the cranium, formed a kind of skull-and-crossbones effect that seemed to warn of danger ahead. Above this point the vegetation changed to a cover of primitive plants. Moss grew in clumps along the stream, freshened by the spray from the rocks, and on an island in the stream hundreds of tan finger-shaped lichens thrust up, each completely hollow. White "reindeer moss" lichen, a staple food of the caribou, spread like foam upon the ground in small billows and tufts. As I climbed higher, these hardy plants disappeared, and there was little except jagged rock that had been heaved from the slopes by frost action. Following a sharp bend in the stream, I emerged into a shadowed open space, a kind of amphitheater, walled with mountain slopes and floored with gravel. Ahead of me loomed the glacier—more gray than white and seemingly more stone than ice, inert, like a great dam blocking the ravine. Rivulets of water raced down its face. Bones—perhaps the remains of Dall sheep killed by either wolves or the arctic winter—lay scattered about on the gravel at my feet.

I was taken aback by the glacier's somberness, unnerved by its size. But I felt a compulsion to see the ice field at the top of the glacier, which I thought I could glimpse if I climbed to the summit of the steep, rocky slope to my right. I started up—and climbed and climbed. Somehow the snag-toothed summit never seemed to get any closer. Fear began to build inside me. I missed Spence. What if he had fallen and bashed his skull in? What if I fell—or started a rockslide? I pivoted, hoping to get some glimpse of him making his way up the ravine and was startled to see how high I had come. At my feet the slope slanted dizzily away. I looked out into space. Mountains rose to taller mountains, blue all over and crested with snow. Any thought I might have had of turning back vanished when it occurred to me that I might be the first person ever to behold this view.

I resumed the climb, grabbing the rocks with both hands and inching upward. But then, probably not 50 feet from the top, I panicked. I had to go back down. Tripping and sliding and stumbling to safety, I came off the slope with joy and a sense of relief. Even the sight of a distant white-bodied jet, tracing two contrails in the cloudless sky, was welcome; I responded to it as though to another human being—I waved at it. Entering the ravine, I once more felt safe. The familiarity of grass under my feet was wonderful. When I reached the spot where I had left my pack, I saw my lunch set out for me by Spence, who had eaten and gone off again to take pictures. What had scared me up on the slope, I think, was the utter impassivity of the glacier and its surroundings. It was as if I had confronted God, and found Him neither loving nor stern, just terribly unconcerned.

JULY 22/From where we camped last night on a stony hummock above three waterfalls it was but a short climb to a plateau where we would have found less rocky ground on which to sleep. But I was too tired to go on—so bushed in fact that in my haste to get into my sleeping bag I left my camera out in the rain all night. The two-mile climb to the glacier yesterday took more energy than I realized, and the hike afterward to this spot, with the worst mosquitoes of the trip, finished me off.

It was still raining when I awoke this morning—and the tent had begun to leak. With only a day's supply of food left we could not wait for the weather to clear; we had to push on. As we sweated our way up to the plateau, I nearly stepped into fresh bear scat. Spence crushed a piece of it between his thumb and forefinger to see if it was still warm. It was. But the bear—which I envisioned waiting for us at the crest —never materialized; perhaps it had taken shelter in the rocks.

The plateau was a realm of its own, a vast, empty place, awash with rain water. Crossing it, I had the feeling of being amid the ruins of a lost civilization. Frost action had heaved many of the rocks into circular arrangements reminiscent of the crumbling foundations of vanished buildings; it had set other rocks in parallel rows, forming paths and roadways. Some rocks stood on end, like tombstones, and some filled mysterious boat-shaped depressions in the ground. Black, ruffled lichens spread concentric circles of patient growth across the weathered rock surfaces. On the soil and gravel beside the rocks lay piles of soaked *Cetraria richardsonii,* a lichen that contracts into a ball as it dries and rolls along with the wind, but when wet unfurls and clings to the ground. Spence thought the soaked lichens looked like heaps of miniature caribou antlers—and indeed they do.

Moving on to another lonesome valley, we walked along the base of a mountain shaped like a massive fortress, complete with parapets and battlements. Atop other mountains stood watchtowerlike outcroppings of weathered stone. The whole place had a sinister aspect, and we were glad to leave it for another much wider valley. There, for the first time in two days, we saw trees—white spruce and cottonwood—and after all the bleakness and starkness they were a welcome sight. We hiked down this valley all afternoon, following a creek much of the way. Off and on we talked about the meal we would eat when we got back to base camp at Last Lake and made ourselves so hungry that we tried to catch a few fish for supper with the gill net we had found in the Air Force box. The water had risen in the creek and become muddied, and the grayling had retreated to the clearer sloughs. Carefully we stretched the net across the mouth of one of these, weighting the bottom end with stones and propping up the top with sticks, forming a kind of fence. Then we marched to the end of the slough and began to beat the water with sticks, hoping to drive the grayling we had seen lurking there toward the net. But the fish had all disappeared.

A test of just how well Spence had been reading our topographic map came in the evening when he announced that we could expect to see a tiny lake at a certain point. But when we arrived at the spot we saw no lake. Had we taken the wrong route? Only after thrashing around in the brush for a while did we find the lake hidden behind raised banks overgrown with bushes.

As Spence reached the lake rim, he threw up his arm and motioned for me to be still. A large bull moose was feeding in the water. We ducked into a clump of dwarf birch and crept toward the unsuspecting animal. We were so excited that at first we did not see another moose partially hidden by a small peninsula jutting out from shore. Both were magnificent specimens, with their black-brown bodies sleek and muscled and their antlers covered with soft velvet. They moved along gracefully, submerging their huge heads in the lake, nipping vegetation from the bottom, then resurfacing, the water crashing off their antlers in thick, noisy streams.

They continued feeding for five minutes or more, unaware of our presence; then as we crawled toward one moose, it heard us and waded to shore. A moment later the other followed. But instead of taking flight, both clambered halfway up a steep bank and stopped, turned and looked at us. They showed no fear—probably they had never seen men before. Only after the moose had satisfied their curiosity (though not ours) did they trot off.

JULY 24/We slept late yesterday—and, as it turned out, this proved a major error. For by the time we got back to the Sheenjek River the rain that had been falling all morning had filled and broadened the river's channels. Spence waded into the swirling cocoa-colored flood and, after taking only a couple of steps, stood thigh deep. We dared not risk a crossing without a rope and poles to steady ourselves—yet our food and life raft lay on the other side.

As we paced the bank, trying to figure out what to do, we heard a plane. Looking up, we saw a floatplane flying toward us. From the insignia on its fuselage, we knew that Averill Thayer had come looking for us. He had told us before we started our expedition that he would be flying in our direction on a trip to Barter Island.

Spence scratched an "F," for food, in the sand, trusting that Thayer would understand that we were out of provisions—separated by the

How Plants Survive on the Tundra

The plants of the Alaskan tundra have survived by adapting themselves to withstand the fierce, arid winds that blow the year round, a winter that gets down to −40° F., and a fleeting summer that gives them only six to nine weeks in which to grow and flower.

The plants have evolved so that they meet such harsh conditions in many ways; the most conspicuous are their small size, compact form, and low growth habit. A salix, or ground willow, for example, spreads low along the ground, rarely rising more than a few inches high but often reaching a breadth of 10 to 15 feet. Other species, among them the moss campion, are tight cushions that are dotted with blossoms; still others, like the buttercup, put forth flowers in snug clusters.

Leaves and stems assist in the plants' struggle to keep warm and retain moisture in a cold, windy climate. Various species, such as the lingonberry, have leaves with leathery or waxy surfaces that retard evaporation. A graceful plant with an ungracious name, the woolly lousewort puts forth hairy insulation on stems and buds that act to hold heat in the plant. As a result of these adaptations, arctic plants exist in microclimates more hospitable than their general environment. In the case of one moss campion, measurements revealed that the temperature inside the plant was 40 degrees warmer than the air around it.

A woolly lousewort wraps its upper leaves in a fibrous muff that gives the plant its name.

Stunted tundra willow hugs the ground to escape the wind.

Moss campion grows and flowers in a heat-conserving mat.

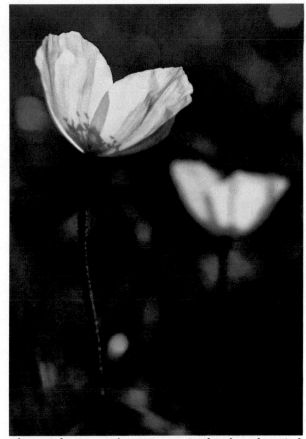

The supple stems of arctic poppies bend to the wind.

Clustered in a tiny bush, buttercups open up toward the sun.

A lingonberry's waxy leaves hold in essential moisture.

river from our supplies at Last Lake—and hoping he could somehow help us. Thayer, circling, tipped his wing and flew off. To our relief, he was back in only half an hour. Thrusting his hand out the window, he dropped a paper bag. Inside were a length of nylon rope and a section torn from a map like ours showing a lake circled with pencil. On the bag he had scribbled, "Have your gear aboard plane. Will leave at lake." We started off, stumbling over the tussocks, and had not gotten far when we saw Thayer returning. Again he dropped a message, this one printed in big letters on the back of his flight map: "Lake no good. Will try river." He flew off, heading downstream, and we saw him circling over a spot about two miles away.

To reach the spot where he touched down, we had to cross what amounted to an obstacle course—a vast flat area paved with tussocks. Thayer had taken off again long before we arrived at the landing site. We could understand his reluctance to linger. Coming down on the river was one thing, getting off in the current another; but somehow he had managed and had piled our food and gear neatly on a big sandbar, and draped the yellow raft over the branches of a willow bush.

Since the valley for hundreds of yards around consisted of bogs and tussocks on which it would have been impossible to pitch a tent, we decided to stay on the sandbar where we were, separated from land by a narrow channel of the Sheenjek. We carried our stuff to a high spot on the bar and again slung the raft over a willow bush, forming a crude shelter. Then we scurried around gathering broken branches and old roots with which to build a fire. But starting a fire in the rain, using wet wood, presented difficulties. Spence cracked the branches open and turned the unsoaked insides down. Slowly the flames grew, providing sufficient heat to dry out the rest of the wood piled on top, and eventually we had a good, though smoky, fire going. We celebrated by breaking into our supplies and eating a big lunch.

Warm and well fed, we were in a better frame of mind to assess our situation—which plainly was not good. The Sheenjek had continued to rise, and the narrow channel between us and the land had grown impressively wide. Spence said he was a poor swimmer, and I can barely swim at all. So neither of us was much inclined to launch our still unproved raft into the raging current. I remembered the survival booklet we had found in the Air Force box and took it from my pack. We opened it to read—and had our first good laugh of the day. "The outdoors is friendly," ran one passage. "Don't be afraid of it. Nature will give you food and drink, warmth and cover if you will take advantage of it. Above all—keep your HEAD." The booklet ended: "Native tribes live for generations in the open air, taking their living from nature. You can do the same. Make the most of every opportunity. Keep cool—and you'll come out of your experience a better man. Best of luck, and remember that courage alone has won many a battle."

We huddled under our shelter throughout the gray night and well into today's gray morning, taking turns tending the fire or dozing. Though the rain stopped around midnight, the river had yet to crest. In a more temperate region the river's rise would have been moderate. But here, because of the permafrost shield, the rain could not soak into the ground—and so had to drain off the land into the streams, creeks and rivers. We watched the water slither toward us, creeping through depressions in the sand, riding over high spots, approaching within a few feet of our boots. Only then did it seem to stop. A short time later we had confirmation that the water was going down: sticks we had driven into the sand earlier to measure its rise began to reappear. Now we had a new dread—of another rainstorm. Out of the south bulging clouds were making their way in our direction. But they passed overhead and the sun came out.

By midafternoon the river had gone down far enough for us to launch the raft. We drifted along with the current, spinning around in it, bouncing over the riffles, swirling by the water-gouged banks where the permafrost could be seen in layers of dirt-colored ice. What luxury to sit back and let the river do the work. Best of all, out on the water we escaped the mosquitoes that emerged with the sun. Except for the trickling of the current, there was no other sound. Then a gull spotted us and, dipping low, began to scream at us. We screamed back—and the bird answered. It kept flying ahead of us; whenever we caught up with it, it circled and regained the lead. Thus it led us on.

JULY 25/Riding the Sheenjek, we stop when and where we want to stop. Today we went ashore to take the lay of the land from a rise and saw, on the opposite side of the river, a female moose with twin calves. They walked as one animal, each in step with the others; then, like a mother and daughters taking the wash down from a clothesline, they moved along a line of willows, reaching up with their heads and delicately nipping buds and leaves from the branches. At another spot farther downstream we surprised two golden eagles sitting on a sandbar. As they flew off, we could see that they were molting: one had a feather missing from each of its wings—the sky showed through the gaps.

We found both feathers on the sandbar, long, strong flight feathers with a glint of gold on them. I kept them.

We liked this area well enough to camp on a hill overlooking the river and several small lakes. The spruces were tasseled with cones on their uppermost branches. Lingonberries, bright red on the sun side, green on the other, lay ripening among the grass and lichens, and blueberries still too tart to eat hung on bushes. From our perch we had every expectation of seeing some wildlife—and we were right. In the evening, through a veil of mosquitoes dangling around our heads, we spotted a male moose near one of the lakes. He advanced toward us, stopped, sniffed, skirted cautiously around some willows, disappeared, then reappeared and sniffed again. At last, apparently convinced that he had traced the source of our strange human smell, he departed, trotting away against a backdrop of mist rising from the valley floor.

JULY 26/After a breakfast of wonderfully sweet grayling, fresh caught from one of the small lakes, we hiked a couple of miles toward a waterfall we could see pouring down the side of a mountain. We had no way of telling how big it really was until we stood below it. The water cascaded from a height of some 2,000 feet, angling through the rocks, rushing in a torrent down to the valley, then flowing toward the Sheenjek with the roar of an express train. We tried climbing to the top of the mountain, but were stopped three quarters of the way up by sheer limestone walls. From here we beheld the same kind of sight that the westward pioneers once witnessed—a land still completely unsullied by man. The spruce below massed into a forest thicker and broader than any we had so far seen on our trip; we were beginning to leave the true Arctic behind us. From our perch on the limestone face of the mountain, we could see, off to our left, the land we had already traversed; we then turned and looked to our right, in the direction of Lobo Lake, where the day after tomorrow our pilot is to pick us up and fly us back to civilization. I want to stay here forever.

JULY 28/Yesterday we were in no hurry to go anywhere. Like Walt Whitman, we loafed and invited our souls. Not until late at night did we board the raft to float the rest of the way down the Sheenjek to Lobo Lake. Everything seemed asleep, even the motionless clouds in the sky, colored gold and salmon pink by the setting sun (and an hour later by the rising sun). As we drifted along the dark brown riverbanks, willow ptarmigan stirred from their slumber to gargle at us, and a loon flapped from the water. Passing a gravel bar, we caught sight of a yearling female moose, standing rigid as a statue among the willows. In the brief hour between sunset and dawn the light turned blue, and a damp chill settled into the raft. We arrived at a bend in the river opposite Lobo Lake, our final destination, at 3 a.m., built a fire to warm ourselves, cooked and ate our supper (we have allowed the rhythm of our needs to overcome habit), pitched our tent and went to sleep.

When we woke this morning, we found the life raft gone. Apparently, in our sleepiness, we had neglected to tie it up securely, and the wind that blew up early in the morning had carried it downstream and tossed it onto a sandbar. Fortunately, Spence was able to retrieve it. Hoping that this was the last of our misadventures, we climbed the pyramid of a hill behind us and sat there in the warm sunlight. The river, snaking down from the north, was bluer than the sky, and the shining green land around it seemed to be drinking in the sun's last bit of warmth. Now, more than ever before, we experienced the spirit of the wilderness—a kind of deep calm and serenity. In two weeks of wandering Spence and I had shed clocks and calendars and gained a sense of nature's timelessness.

What we had so blessedly escaped in the wilderness—the pressure of time, the press of people living and working close together—came flooding back on our return to Fairbanks. There Spence and his blond wife Randy make their home; there I was to emplane for New York. A Gold Rush town that became a city, Fairbanks encroaches ever more into the spruce forest that rings it. The once-pure Chena River, which flows through the downtown section of the city, is now polluted. During winter the air contains dangerously high levels of lead and carbon monoxide, emitted by the hundreds of automobile engines that people leave running for hours to keep them warm. In so big a state as Alaska such problems are happily still only local ones. But for how long? How long before the blighting effects of civilization, now manifest in much of the rest of the United States, hit the north? Will the frontier spirit that conquered the forests, tamed the deserts, harnessed the rivers in the Lower 48—and left only 2 per cent of the land wild—also prevail here? Some say yes. Those Alaskans who love their state might say no. They would not be living here—participating, as one Alaskan has put it, in a legend—if they did not care deeply about wilderness.

At the same time they are realists. They know that they must pay more for goods and services than other Americans, that they must create from scratch the costly trappings of American life, including schools, libraries, roads and hospitals. They cannot be blamed if they discern a way out of their economic dilemma through their natural resources—all those fabled riches that supposedly lie locked up underground and need only to be tapped to make the state wealthy. Thus some Alaskans, believing that part of the wilderness is expendable (though never saying which part), see the future in terms of new settlements, new roads, new mines and new oilfields. But other Alaskans, understanding all too well what it would mean to surrender the wilderness piecemeal for the sake of development, joined a large coalition of conservation-oriented organizations that helped to shepherd the 1980 Alaska Lands Act through Congress. The act provides federal protection for enormous chunks of wilderness, but much of the state is still available to developers.

Already oil has begun to change the Alaskan wilderness, and there is no telling how drastically it will affect the landscape in the years to come. Geologists believe that oil- and gas-bearing strata may underlie one third of the state and most of its coastal waters. The proved oil reserves of the 200-square-mile Prudhoe Bay field on the North Slope come to about eight billion barrels, while the potential for the entire North Slope, a region about the size of Italy, is estimated at as high as 100 billion barrels. In southern Alaska, on the Kenai Peninsula and in Cook Inlet, wells produced close to 950 million barrels in a little more than two decades after beginning production. Other discoveries could come at any time and in any place, particularly in the coastal region of the Arctic National Wildlife Refuge.

So far oil has meant a desecration of the wilderness. The federal government became the first offender in the 1940s when it launched extensive oil explorations of the North Slope. Tractor treads ran hogwild over the delicate tundra; the wounds they inflicted have not yet healed and may never entirely heal. To allow geologists to take soundings for oil, the top layer of insulating vegetation had to be scraped off in some areas, thus exposing the underlying permafrost; as the sun's rays melted the permafrost, canals formed, eroding the soil. Crews strewed the ground with litter, and much of it is still there today. Things deteriorate slowly in the Arctic.

Then came the oil companies. When large-scale drilling operations began in 1968, workers removed tons of gravel from river beds and offshore barrier reefs to use in construction of roads and airstrips, and as fill for grading the sites of camps, supply depots and drilling rigs. In

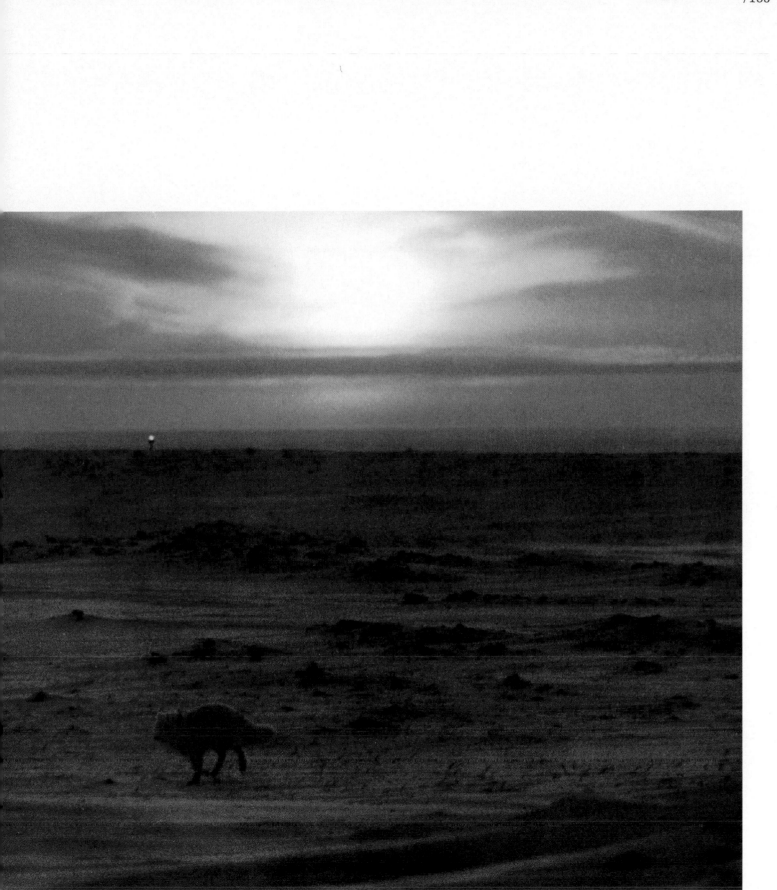

A tundra-prowling arctic fox, protected against the Alaskan winter by its dense white fur, gives a wide berth to a North Slope oil rig.

removing the gravel they risked ruining the spawning grounds of arctic fish. Some companies bulldozed sand dunes that had long been denning sites for arctic foxes and used the cleared areas for garbage disposal. The refuse eventually drew scavengers, among them grizzlies, wolves and wolverines; some were shot by the crewmen as nuisances. Legal and illegal hunting put the wildlife under still more pressure.

The oil companies, prodded by conservationists, have since undertaken serious efforts to make their operations ecologically and esthetically sounder. Both the federal government and the state of Alaska have laid down rules restricting the use of wheeled and tracked vehicles on the tundra—at least in summer, when the surface has thawed. But no one knows how much irreparable damage already may have been done, largely because no one knows exactly what this portion of the North Slope was like before development. Nor does anyone know how much the animals living there may eventually suffer from the loss of rangeland and breeding sites to expanding oil operations. Dr. Weeden has pointed out that nobody ever bothers to study what a wild area is like, or how it will suffer from man's intrusion, until man has already invaded the region and done his inevitable damage. Only then do people become alarmed. Their concern may be timely enough to be effective in preventing further damage; but awareness seldom comes soon enough to forestall encroachment altogether. As a result, some basic questions of arctic ecology are still to be answered.

The worst threat to Alaska's wilderness so far was posed by the 800-mile pipeline that the oil companies began to build in 1974—originally most of it underground—from the Arctic all the way to the ice-free port of Valdez, on Alaska's southern coast. In their haste to launch the project the companies ordered all the required pipe before conducting engineering studies of the varied regions through which the line would pass. But one did not need to be an engineer to doubt the wisdom of burying pipe full of warm oil in ground that is partly underlaid by permafrost and located over an earthquake fault. The prospect generated such a public uproar in Alaska and elsewhere that the companies reconsidered their plans. The Department of the Interior, the agency responsible for approving the pipeline—the route cuts across three mountain ranges and 350 rivers and streams, much of it on federally owned land—then specified that about half of the line would have to be placed above ground, both to avoid melting the permafrost and to minimize the chances of the pipe's rupturing under earthquake stress. The department also stipulated that the companies had to provide for the protection of fish-spawning areas and establish controls to prevent pipeline spills and the pollution that might be caused by pipeline crews. A further stipulation was that the companies had to provide crossings over the pipe for caribou and other large animals—a requirement that baffled engineers and biologists alike, since no one could predict whether the caribou would even try to use the crossing devices. Indeed, since the pipeline and its service road were completed in June 1977, the caribou crossings have been largely ignored by the animals, which prefer to walk under the pipe rather than over it.

Before other oil and natural gas reserves are tapped and other pipelines are built there is time in which to answer many of the nagging questions of arctic ecology and to plan for the careful development of all of Alaska's resources. Among the many thoughtful people who have considered the price of progress in the north is Dr. Weeden. He sees the need for the state to make use of its resources, but on his list of resources wilderness ranks as high as oil. Perhaps it is fitting that in a book about the Alaskan wilderness Weeden, an Alaskan, should have the last word. He states the case eloquently:

"The world needs an embodiment of the frontier mythology, the sense of horizons unexplored, the mystery of uninhabited miles. It needs a place where wolves stalk . . . because a land that can produce a wolf is a healthy, robust and perfect land. The world desperately needs a place to stand under a bright auroral curtain on a winter's evening, in awe of the cosmic cold and silence. But more than these things the world needs to know that there is a place where men live amidst a balanced interplay of the goods of technology and the fruits of Nature. Unless we can prove that a modern society can thrive in harmony with the land, the bits of wildness we salvage in Alaska will be nothing more than curious artifacts in the sad museum of mankind."

A Land of Enormous Vistas

PHOTOGRAPHS BY DEAN BROWN

To make the most of five weeks in the Alaskan wilderness, photographer Dean Brown planned, and then followed, a careful itinerary. Hopscotching by plane, he stopped to photograph areas chosen as prime examples of Alaska's highly varied terrain. He was particularly drawn to the Glacier Bay and Mount Katmai regions along the southern coast, and there he concentrated his camera explorations.

It was at Glacier Bay that Brown was first struck by Alaska's immensity. "Almost everywhere I looked," he said, "mountains stretched away to a long, sharp-edged horizon, and the enormous vistas made me realize how far I was from the nearest pocket of civilization." His feeling of isolation deepened as he flew north and was at its most intense when he landed on the vast marshy flats of the North Slope, where permafrost creates an endless mosaic of random polygons (page 175). "This plain," Brown said, "seemed to me the most desolate place on earth; here the sense of space is almost oppressive."

But the brute power of Alaska's landscape was summed up for Brown in the massive ice walls of Glacier Bay. To photograph the face of Plateau Glacier, which loomed ponderously at the water's edge, he approached it with great caution in a boat. In the summer weather the ice wall was crumbling dangerously, and so Brown remained at a respectful distance, narrowing the gap with a telescopic lens. As an unexpected bonus, the picture (right) caught a flight of Arctic terns flashing as they dived for the fish stirred up by splashes of falling ice.

Though a heavy overcast often mantled the southern coast, Brown found that it lent a white glow to the atmosphere, creating effects that more than made up for the loss of pure light. Fog and mist were even more spectacular, as Brown learned one day after he had left Glacier Bay and flown to the Mount Katmai region, more than 700 miles away on the Alaska Peninsula. Exploring the huge interior of Katmai crater, he was admiring the crater's lake when he realized that a thick fog was rolling in. Quickly he climbed the snowclad inner slope of the crater and aimed his camera up at the sky. In the photograph on pages 178 and 179 the crater's rim stands out sharply against the luminous fog; despite the solidity of the volcanic scarp at left, the eye is led to what seems the very edge of the earth itself.

A GLACIER'S CRUMBLING FACE, GLACIER BAY

THE FAIRWEATHER RANGE, SEEN FROM GLACIER BAY

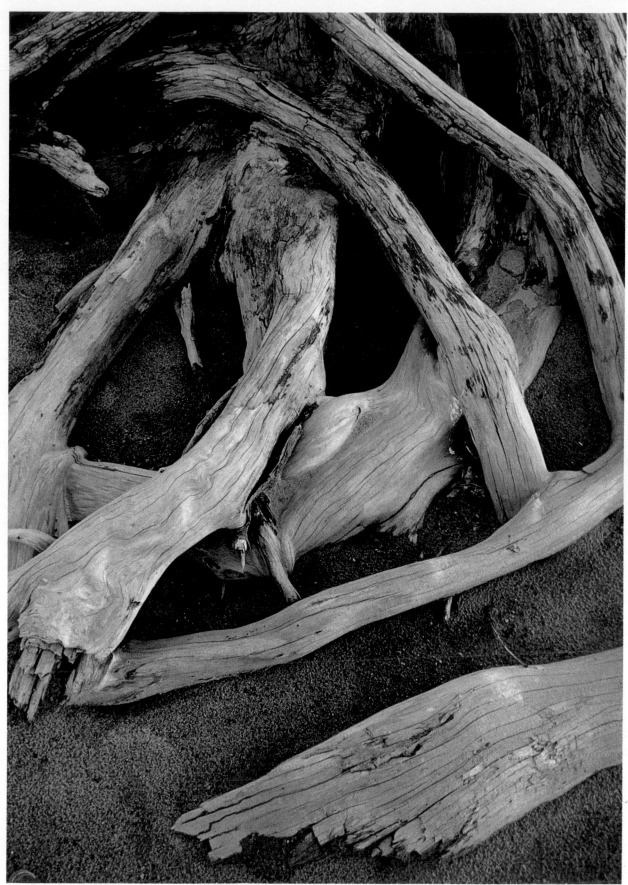

ANCIENT WOOD, PRESERVED BY A PASSING GLACIER

MIDNIGHT ON THE TUNDRA IN DENALI NATIONAL PARK AND PRESERVE

A MOUNTAIN VALLEY IN THE KATMAI REGION, STRIPED WITH SUMMER SNOW

PERMAFROST PATTERNS ON THE NORTH SLOPE TUNDRA

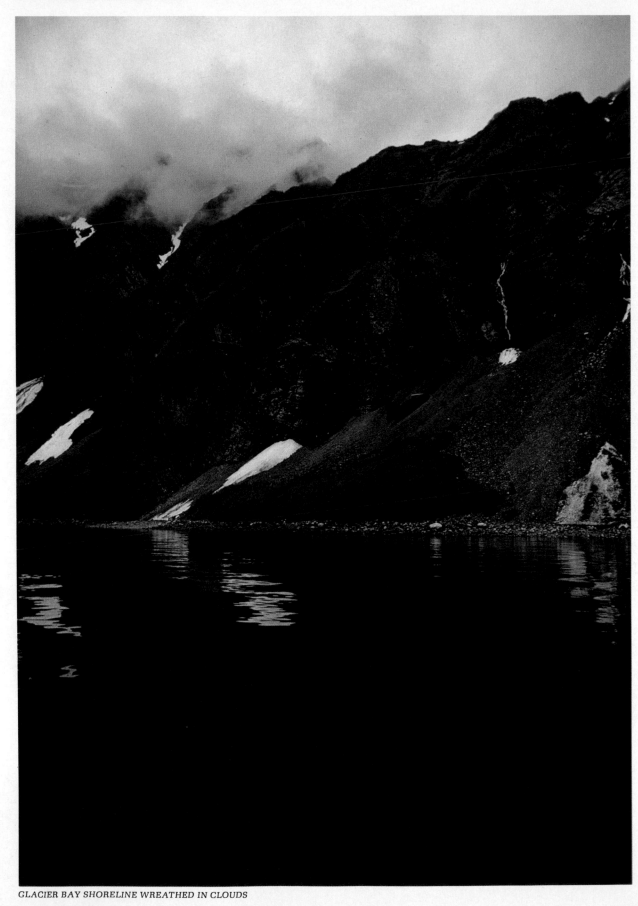

GLACIER BAY SHORELINE WREATHED IN CLOUDS

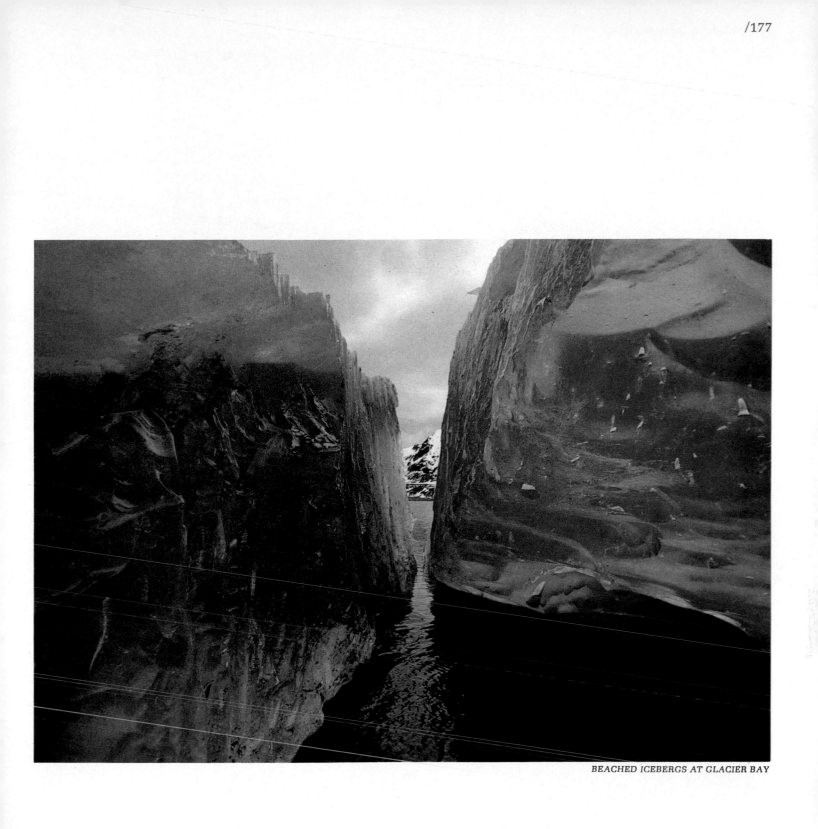

BEACHED ICEBERGS AT GLACIER BAY

INSIDE KATMAI CRATER

Bibliography

Bee, James W., and E. Raymond Hall, *Mammals of Northern Alaska.* University of Kansas, 1956.

Berry, William D., *Deneki: An Alaskan Moose.* The Macmillan Company, 1965.

Bohn, Dave, *Glacier Bay, the Land and the Silence.* Sierra Club, 1967.

Brower, Kenneth, *Earth and the Great Weather: The Brooks Range.* McCall Publishing Company, 1971.

Brown, Tom, *Oil on Ice.* Sierra Club, 1971.

Crisler, Lois, *Arctic Wild.* Harper and Brothers, 1958.

Douglas, William O., *My Wilderness: The Pacific West.* Pyramid Publications, 1960.

Dufresne, Frank, *No Room for Bears.* Holt, Rinehart and Winston, 1965.

Gabrielson, Ira N., and Frederick C. Lincoln, *The Birds of Alaska.* Stackpole Company and the Wildlife Management Institute, 1959.

Gohl, Heinrich, *Alaska.* Rand McNally and Company, 1970.

Griggs, Robert F., *The Valley of Ten Thousand Smokes.* The National Geographic Society, 1922.

Gruening, Ernest, *Lonely Wonders of Katmai, Alaska.* National Geographic, Vol. 123, No. 6, June 1963.

Hansen, Henry P., ed., *Arctic Biology.* Oregon State University Press, 1967.

Heller, Christine, *Wild Flowers of Alaska.* Graphic Arts Center, Portland, Oregon, 1966.

Heller, Herbert L., ed., *Sourdough Sagas.* World Publishing Company, 1967.

Henning, Bob, ed., *The Milepost.* Alaska Northwest Publishing Co., 1976.

Kelsall, John P., *The Migratory Barren-Ground Caribou of Canada.* Department of Indian Affairs and Northern Development, Canadian Wildlife Service, 1968.

Kimble, George H. T., and Dorothy Good, eds., *Geography of the Northlands.* American Geographical Society and J. Wiley, 1955.

Leopold, A. Starker, and F. Fraser Darling, *Wildlife in Alaska.* Ronald Press Company, 1953.

Marshall, Robert, *Alaska Wilderness: Exploring the Central Brooks Range.* University of California Press, 1970.

Martin, George C., *The Recent Eruption of Katmai Volcano in Alaska.* The National Geographic Magazine, Vol. 24, No. 2, February 1913.

Mech, L. David, *The Wolf: The Ecology and Behavior of an Endangered Species.* Natural History Press, 1970.

Miller, Mike, *Off the Beaten Path in Alaska.* Alaskabooks (Number 101), 1970.

Murie, Adolph, *Birds of Mount McKinley National Park Alaska.* Mount McKinley Natural History Association, 1963.

Murie, Adolph, *A Naturalist in Alaska.* The Devin-Adair Company, 1961.

Murie, Adolph, *The Wolves of Mount McKinley.* Fauna of the National Parks of the United States, Fauna Series No. 5, U.S. Government Printing Office, 1944.

Potter, Louise, *Wild Flowers along Mt. McKinley Park Road.* Privately printed, 1969.

Pruitt, William O., Jr., *Animals of the North.* Harper and Row, 1960.

Riley, Laura and William, *Guide to the National Wildlife Refuges.* Anchor Press/Doubleday, 1979.

Smith, Richard A., and the Editors of TIME-LIFE BOOKS, *The Frontier States: Hawaii and Alaska.* TIME-LIFE BOOKS, 1968.

Staender, Gilbert and Vivian, *Adventures with Arctic Wildlife.* The Caxton Printers, 1970.

Stonehouse, Bernard, *Animals of the Arctic: The Ecology of the Far North.* Holt, Rinehart and Winston, 1971.

U.S. Geological Survey, Howel Williams, ed., *Landscapes of Alaska: Their Geologic Evolution.* University of California Press, 1958.

Wilkinson, Douglas, *The Arctic Coast.* N.S.L. National Science of Canada Ltd., 1970.

Acknowledgments

The author and editors of this book wish to thank the following: Gilbert Blinn, Katmai National Park and Preserve; Ernest J. Borgman, National Park Service, Pacific Northwest Region, Seattle; Tim Bradner, British Petroleum Alaska, Anchorage; James Brooks, Anchorage; Dolly Connelly, Port Townsend, Washington; R. N. de Armond, Juneau; Christine Enright, U.S. Fish and Wildlife Service, Washington, D.C.; Robert B. Forbes, Professor of Geology, Geophysical Institute, University of Alaska, College; Ed Fortier and staff of Alaska Magazine, Edmonds, Washington; Joan Gidlund, National Park Service, Alaska Region, Anchorage; Richard J. Gordon, Juneau; Gordon C. Haber, Department of Zoology, University of British Columbia, Vancouver; David Hickok, University of Alaska Sea Grant Program, Anchorage; Sidney S. Horenstein, Department of Invertebrate Paleontology, The American Museum of Natural History, New York City; Robert E. Howe, Superintendent, Glacier Bay National Park and Preserve; Celia Hunter, Camp Denali, College; Loyal J. Johnson, Alaska Department of Fish and Game, Fairbanks; Charles V. Janda, Glacier Bay National Park and Preserve; A. Durand Jones, National Park Service, Washington, D.C.; David C. Klinger, U.S. Fish and Wildlife Service, Washington, D.C.; John J. Koranda, University of California, Livermore; Spencer Linderman, University of Alaska, College; Duncan Morrow, National Park Service, Washington, D.C.; Bruce Paige, Glacier Bay National Park and Preserve; Larry G. Pardue, Plant Information Specialist, New York Botanical Garden, Bronx; Robert A. Rausch, Alaska Department of Fish and Game, Anchorage; J. Thomas Ritter, National Park Service, Pacific Northwest Division, Seattle; Vernon Ruesch, Superintendent, Denali National Park and Preserve; Roy Sanborn, Denali National Park and Preserve; Tony Smith, Alaska Department of Fish and Game, Fairbanks; Gregory Streveler, Glacier Bay National Park and Preserve; Averill Thayer, U.S. Fish and Wildlife Service, Fairbanks; Charles Towill, British Petroleum Alaska, Anchorage; Will Troyer, U.S. Fish and Wildlife Service, Anchorage; Skip Wallen, Juneau; Robert Weeden, Professor of Wildlife Management, University of Alaska, College; Ginny Wood, Camp Denali, College; Ian A. Worley, Assistant Professor of Botany, University of Vermont, Burlington.

Picture Credits

Sources for the pictures in this book are shown below. Credits for the pictures from left to right are separated by commas; from top to bottom they are separated by dashes.

Cover—Pete K. Martin. Front end papers 1, 2—M. Woodbridge Williams, National Park Service. Front end paper 3, page 1—Pete K. Martin. 2, 3—Grossman-Granger Productions, Ltd. 4, 5—Susan Rayfield. 6, 7—Dean Brown. 8, 9—Tee Balog. 10, 11—Pete K. Martin. 12, 13—Gerald R. Brimacombe. 18, 19—Map by R. R. Donnelley Cartographic Services. 24, 25—Tim J. Setnicka. 30, 31—La Roche Photo Seattle, American Geographical Society. 36, 37—Ed Cooper. 43—Map by R. R. Donnelley Cartographic Services. 44, 45—Charles V. Janda. 50, 51—Dean Brown. 54—Dean Brown. 56—Charles V. Janda, Dale Brown (2)—Dale Brown except center Susan Rayfield. 57—Dale Brown, Dean Brown—Dean Brown, Joseph A. Witt. 60—Charlie Ott from National Audubon Society. 61—Kenneth W. Fink. 62, 63—Ben Strickland from Van Cleve Photography. 68, 69, 70—Dean Brown. 71—Dean Brown, Kenneth W. Fink. 72—Dale Brown—Dean Brown. 73—Dale Brown except center Dean Brown. 74, 75—Dean Brown. 76, 77—Susan Rayfield—Dale Brown, Dean Brown. 81—Map by R. R. Donnelley Cartographic Services. 86, 87: Dean Brown. 92, 93—Tee Balog, Michael C. T. Smith from National Audubon Society. 94, 95—Tee Balog, Fritz Goro for LIFE. 99, 100, 101—Dean Brown. 102, 103—Dale Brown. 104—Dean Brown. 105—Dale Brown. 106, 107—Dean Brown. 111—Map by R. R. Donnelley Cartographic Services. 116, 117—Dean Brown. 122, 123—Charlie Ott from National Audubon Society, Kenneth W. Fink. 124, 125—Willis Peterson, W. E. Ruth. 130, 131—Dean Brown. 136, 137—Gordon Haber except right Fritz Goro for LIFE. 138, 139—Gordon Haber. 143—Map by R. R. Donnelley Cartographic Services. 144, 145—Dale Brown. 148—James W. Helmericks. 152-153—Bud Helmericks, Tim J. Setnicka. 158, 159—Gilbert F. Staender, Kenneth Roberson (2)—John Milton, John Milton—Charlie Ott. 164, 165—Grossman-Granger Productions, Ltd. 169 through 179—Dean Brown.

Index

*Numerals in italics indicate a photograph
or drawing of the subject mentioned.*